The Epic Trivia Quiz & Fun Facts Bundle

Random Knowledge and Awesome Trivia
Questions - For Laughter at Family Road
Trips, Trivia Night or the Bathroom

ISBN: 979-8-518596-05-4 (Paperback)
ISBN: 978-1-953991-02-7 (Hardback)

Cover design by 100Covers
Interior design by FormattedBooks

FUNTASTIC!

507 Fantastic Fun Facts

Crazy Trivia Knowledge for Adults and Kids Including
Information About Animals, Space and More

ZACH OLSON

Table of Contents

Introduction

Do you want to learn new trivia and start engaging discussions with your family and friends? Or are you looking for a book that will entertain your child and help them build a love for reading? Maybe you just want a funnier life and a great read for the bathroom. It doesn't matter how old you are or what interests you generally have, this book can be enjoyed by everyone.

In *Funtastic!* you will learn 507 fantastic fun facts. These random facts about animals, science, records, money and more will entertain anyone reading them. Even if you normally are not that bookish, you can find pleasure in reading these facts. This book can help everyone start reading and establish a love for learning new things. You will laugh about the absurd facts and learn something valuable from the others. In addition, the quiz at the end is challenging and will make you curious to learn more!

About the Author

Hi, my name is Zach, and I'm a proud "hodophile." If you don't know what that means, here comes the first fact: A hodophile is someone who loves to travel. In my opinion, traveling is a must. It urges you to do things you otherwise never would. Getting out of that comfort zone is what makes your life exciting and adventurous. On the other hand, traveling also allows you to take a break, relax and appreciate your life.

Thinking about life enables new perspectives and opens one's mind. By meeting new people from various places, different world views come together. The diversity of these cultures leads to one of the most important factors of traveling: learning. It's overwhelming how many skills or amount of knowledge we can accumulate while visiting foreign countries and living unfamiliar lifestyles.

I have been traveling around the world for over a year and learned plenty of new things. Thanks to all the experiences, there's always something exciting to talk about, be it a cool story, a great joke, or an interesting fact. I always get great feedback on the facts I tell, and they often result in heavy but interesting discussions. That's why I started a list with funny and exciting knowledge that ended up becoming this book.

Hopefully, this inspires you to be more curious about life, develop a joy of discovery, and maybe even start traveling around the world.

So let's dive right into it...

·1·

ANIMAL KINGDOM PART 1

Let the journey begin! Millions of years before humans evolved from apes, animals had already conquered the earth. Many of them, like dinosaurs and mammoths, have died out, but others survived and developed until present day.

Nowadays, most households have a pet; in the US, the pet ownership rate is 67%. It's no coincidence the dog is called "man's best friend." This shows the popularity of animals in the modern world. And if somebody doesn't have a pet or just wants to see some more exotic animals, they can simply visit the zoo next door. Zoos achieve something extraordinary; animals that would live huge distances away from each other are now neighbors. Lions living in the desert, fishes living in the ocean, monkeys housing in the jungle, and much more – we can visit them all in just one hour of strolling around.

Although we can see many different animals, they only represent a fraction of all the species existing on this planet. It's impossible to say how many there are; some of them are living in inaccessible places and some are too small to be found. Overall, it's just insane to count every single animal on the planet. Scientists estimate that around 1 to 2 million species exist. How many of them do you know? And what do you know about them? In this chapter, you are definitely going to learn something new about these various creatures.

#1 If you keep a goldfish in the dark, it will become pale.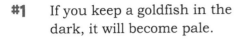

#2 Foxes have whiskers on their legs. They help them keep their bearings, especially when it's dark outside.

#3 The *Goliath Frog* is the most giant frog in the world and can grow up to 12.5 inches (32cm) in length and weigh up to 7.2 pounds (3.3kg).

#4 On a flight in the Congo, a crocodile escaped from a duffel bag, causing everybody to run to the front of the plane. Out of balance, the plane crashed, leaving only one survivor.

#5 Reindeer are able to see UV light.

#6 *Turkey Vultures* use defensive vomit. They can spit their vomit up to 10 feet (3 m).

#7 A swan, which is the largest member of the goose and duck family, has over 25,000 feathers on its body.

#8 The group of multiple whales is called a *pod*.

- -

#9   Bumblebees have hair on their eyes.

- -

#10   The heart of a giraffe pumps twice as hard as a cow's heart, in order to get blood to its brain.

#11   The *mongoose*, that weasel-like creature, is one of those rare animals that is immune to a snake's venom.

#12   Dogs can be allergic to humans – mainly their dander.

#13   Except for a few organs, caterpillars liquefy almost completely while undergoing metamorphosis.

#14   The *Cesky Terrier* (around 350 of them exist in total, worldwide) is the rarest breed of dog in the world.

#15   After just a few hours of being born, baby horses can walk and run.

#16 The *Saltwater Crocodile* has the highest bite force of any animal. However, the muscles to open the mouth are weak. You could shut its mouth with a couple layers of duct tape.

#17 *Pitbulls* are highly ranked among the most affectionate and least aggressive dogs. They are only aggressive when trained as such (usually for illegal dogfighting).

#18 Some butterfly species are speedy; the *Skipper Butterfly* can fly faster than a horse can run.

#19 If rabbits are approached by a predator when they are unaware, they can be literally "scared to death."

#20 *"Ear furnishings"* are those cute furry bits inside a cat's ear. They help them to hear well and ensure that dirt doesn't go inside.

#21 If a snake has its head chopped off, that clipped-off head can still bite and unleash a massive amount of venom.

#22 The only species of spider classified as vegetarian is the *Bagheera Kiplingi Spider,* which was discovered in the 1800s.

- -

#23 Kangaroos keep growing until they die. They are the world's largest marsupial.

- -

#24 Jellyfish are considered biologically immortal. They don't age and will only die if they are killed.

#25 Probably, young *Tyrannosaurus Rex* had a thin coat of downy feathers to stay warm. As they got older, they did not need them due to their size.

#26 Owls have specialized feathers. The edges protrude out to dissipate airflow, which means they can fly silently and are very deadly hunters.

#27 Waxworms can eat and break down plastic bags. This was found out by an amateur beekeeper and a group of scientists. The settings of the stomach of a waxworm can be recreated to dispose of plastic bags and bottles safely.

#28 If their mate dies, elephants can die of a broken heart.

#29 The cat's front paws are different from the back ones. On the front, they have five toes but only four on the back.

#30 Dolphins can be used for locating underwater mines and rescuing lost naval swimmers. Both the *US Army* and *Soviet militaries* have trained dolphins for this purpose.

#31 *Roselle* is a guide dog who led her blind owner down 78 flights of stairs during 9/11. They both safely made it out, even though the descent took about an hour.

#32 Ant queens may live for up to 30 years.

#33 The bigger the brain of an animal, the longer they will yawn. An animal's yawn is based on how large its brain is.

#34 *Bookworm* is a general name for insects that bore holes in books. Paper lice, for example, feed on microscopic mold in poorly kept books.

#35 *John Quincy Adams* kept a pet alligator in one of the White House bathtubs and enjoyed showing it off. He got it from a French general.

#36   *Dingoes*, which are about the same size as a *Springer Spaniel*, are brave enough to attack an adult kangaroo when hunting in packs.

#37   In the US, approximately 1,000,000 dogs are named as the heirs of their owners' wills.

#38   The hugest species of hamster is the "European" or "Common hamster" (*Cricetus cricetus*). It has a length of up to 34 cm (13.3 in), plus a tail length of 6 cm (2.4 in), yielding a total length of up to 40 cm (15.7 in). It can live for eight years.

#39   Gorillas are able to catch human colds and other illnesses.

#40   Researchers found that the loudness of a monkey is relative to the size of its testicles — the smaller the testicles, the louder the monkey.

#41   Zebras only have one toe on each foot.

#42 The *Bumblebee Bat* weighs about the same as a US dime. It's the world's smallest mammal. Native to Myanmar and Thailand, these bats are endangered.

#43 The national animal of Scotland is the unicorn.

#44 Studies have proven that llamas can be used as guards against coyote attacks on sheep herds. Just one llama is an effective protector and able to kill the attacking coyotes.

· 2 ·

WORLD AND NATURE

After observing the animals inhabiting this world, it's time to look at the wonderful planet we are all living on. 299 million years ago, all of the earth's landmass formed the supercontinent *Pangea*. Over the years, different landmasses broke apart. They episodically and slowly constituted the continents we now know. This separation and isolation of continents is why they all are unique: different continents, different landscapes, different climates. But also diverse countries, populations, languages and more have developed. It's incredible how the earth has evolved, but still remains the same.

"See the world like an artist" is one of my favorite sayings, be it the mountains, the ancient sights, or the extraordinary design of a leaf. We tend to forget the beauty of the earth, instead of being grateful for this artwork of nature. Also, the accomplishments of humankind are incredible. We have built breathtaking constructions in impossible places on the earth, and multiple populations established various cultures, cities, and countries.

To this date, 195 different countries exist. It's so exciting to explore all these foreign places and experience their cultures. Now, you can discover some interesting facts about this world.

#45 In China, there's a series of underground tunnels running 3,000 miles (4,800 km) long.

#46 In Australia, there are nearly twice as many kangaroos as there are humans.

#47 In a few *Appalachian forests*, some fireflies glow blue instead of flashing yellow.

#48 In Scotland you can travel over the same viaduct as the *Hogwarts Express.*

#49 The only continent turtles don't live on is Antarctica.

#50 Great Britain is connected to continental Europe by an area of land called "Doggerland." In 6500-6200 BC, it was flooded by rising sea-levels, turning Great Britain into an island.

#51 *Lake Superior* (Canada and US) contains 10% of the world's freshwater. It is as big as South Carolina and includes 2,900 cubic miles (12,090 km^3) of water.

#52 Only 45% of the London Underground is under the ground.

#53 Switzerland has one of the highest gun ownership rates in the world, but violent, gun-related street crime is extremely rare. In an average year, for every 200,000 of the population, there is only 1 gun murder (in the US: 24).

#54 In Indiana, there is a town called *Santa Claus*.

#55 Japan may be the cleanest country. For 12 years of school life, cleaning time is a part of the students' daily schedule, and Japanese people rarely leave rubbish on the streets.

#56 There is a Japanese village called *Nagoro* which has 35 inhabitants, but over 350 scarecrows!

#57 In Cambodia, people train rats to sniff out landmines. They can clear 200 square meters (2,000 square feet) in less than 35 minutes, which usually takes 2-3 days with a de-miner.

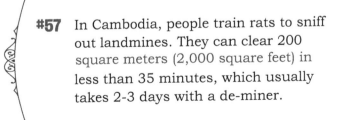

#58 The spectacular *Great Wall of China* is 21,196 km (13,170 mi) long.

#59 Sweden is the country with the most islands in the world. It has 221,800 islands.

#60 Once, Madagascar was an area for lemurs the size of today's gorillas.

#61 Over a million people live in nuclear bunkers underneath the streets of Beijing.

#62 The *Leaning Tower of Pisa* got its title because of the soft soil it's built on – This smooth soil also protected it from at least 4 powerful earthquakes.

#63 *Pig Beach* is an uninhabited island in the Bahamas which is populated entirely by swimming pigs.

#64 The German highway (called *Autobahn*) is famous for not having any speed limits. Although, in reality, around 30% of the roads do have limitations.

#65 It takes longer to drown in salt water than in freshwater. This may be the reason that around 90% of drownings occur in freshwater.

#66 Sudan has 255 pyramids. That's more than any other country. This even outnumbers Egyptian pyramids by twice the number.

#67 Probably the most widely used sign for medical assistance actually is the *Swiss flag* (white cross on red background). The reverse version (red cross on white background) would be correct, as it's the symbol of the *Red Cross*.

#68 Dinosaurs lived on every continent when they roamed the earth, including Antarctica.

#69 The *Great Pyramid of Giza* has 8 sides, rather than 4. All the other pyramids have just 4 sides.

#70 All the paint on the *Eiffel Tower* weighs as much as 10 elephants. It gets repainted every 7 years without closing to the public.

#71 Iceland does not have a railway system.

#72 The quietest room in the world is located in Minnesota. It is measured in negative decibels – so low that you can hear your heart beating.

#73 Over 65,000 pairs of *white-capped albatross* live on an island in New Zealand called "Disappointment Island."

#74 China is spending $3 billion to build panda-shaped solar farms to get more young people interested in renewable energy.

#75 Between North and South Korea lies 155 miles (250 km) of no man's land where hundreds of rare animal species thrive.

#76 *Monowi* is a town in Nebraska with a population of 1. The only resident is a woman who is the Mayor, Bartender and Librarian.

#77 The world's only country named after a woman is *Saint Lucia*.

#78 *Forrest Fenn*, who is an art dealer and author, hid a treasure chest in the Rocky Mountains worth over 1 million dollars. It still has not been discovered. (Update: *Fenn* announced the treasure was found in 2020)

#79 *Maine* is the only state in the United States that has a one-syllable name.

#80 The full name of *Los Angeles* is "El Pueblo de Nuestra Senora la Reina de los Angeles de Porciuncula".

#81 On the 18th of February 1979, it snowed in the *Sahara Desert* for 30 minutes.

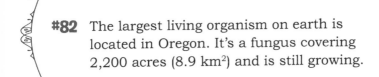

#82 The largest living organism on earth is located in Oregon. It's a fungus covering 2,200 acres (8.9 km^2) and is still growing.

#83 A tsunami caused by an underwater earthquake can travel as fast as a jet plane.

#84 Every minute there are 2,000
thunderstorms on earth.

#85 In Iceland, ice caves exist that have hot springs.

#86 In one year, over 1,200 tornadoes
strike American soil.

#87 *Yuma* (Arizona) is the sunniest place on
earth. It gets over 4,000 hours of sunshine
a year (average 11 hours daily). The least
sunny location is the *South Pole*, where the
sun only shines on 182 days of the year.

#88 A flash of lightning is five times
hotter than the sun.

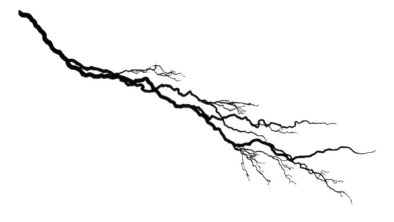

#89 Water covers 70% of the earth.

#90 Only 3% of the water on the earth is fresh, the other 97% is salted.

#91 In Australia's *Daintree Rainforest* grows a tree called the "Idiot Fruit."

#92 *Killer Whales,* also known as *Orcas,* aren't even whales. They are a type of dolphin and the hugest breed of dolphins in existence.

#93 Around 48% of the population in Uganda is under 15 years old.

- -

#94 Nearly 3% of the ice in Antarctic glaciers is penguin urine.

- -

· 3 ·

SPACE

If you think about it, this huge earth we are living on is only a tiny piece of a much bigger unit, the universe. It seems endless, and this is what makes it so fascinating. Many kids dream of becoming an astronaut, being able to float in space and making happy air jumps on the moon. But by seeing the earth from the perspective of an astronaut, we get a better understanding of how little our world is compared to the whole.

Our solar system contains 8 planets (Mercury, Venus, Earth, Mars, Jupiter, Saturn, Uranus and Neptune), without counting dwarf planets. And that's just the beginning because not only the sun (which is a star if you didn't know), but nearly all stars have planets in their own solar systems. And a large part of them are likely to have more planets than our sun. Looking to the night sky, we realize this enormous amount of stars and, therefore, the even bigger number of existing planets. We're talking about trillions of planets in our galaxy alone, and our galaxy isn't the only one in the universe. At least 200 billion other galaxies are out there!

Scientists concluded that this giant universe is filled with around 10^{25} planets. For those wondering, this number is called *ten septillion* and looks like this: 10,000,000,000,000,000,000,000,000. With continuing research, that number is going to become more accurate, but don't get lost in the numbers. What we are looking for on these planets is water and signs of life; that's where the interesting part begins.

#95 On Neptune, each day lasts for around 16 hours and 6 minutes.

#96 A booklet was written explaining how to observe Ramadan while in orbit because a Muslim astronaut had trouble fasting for Ramadan in space.

#97 Spacesuits take 5,000 hours to make, cost 1 million dollars, weigh about 110 pounds (50 kg), and have 11 layers of material.

#98 The first permanent crew inhabiting the *International Space Station (ISS)* started in 2000.

#99 The first soft drink ever consumed in space was *Coca-Cola*.

#100 The tallest mountain in our solar system, *Olympus Mons* (on planet Mars), is 3 times higher than Mount Everest.

#101 There is a *geocache* on the International Space Station. It was placed in 2008.

#102 The first game played in space was *Starcraft* – Daniel Barry took it with him in 1999, on the Space Shuttle mission STS-96.

#103 Russia has the most human-made satellites in orbit (1,324). In total, 2,271 satellites exist, and the US is in second place with 658 satellites.

#104 An 11-year-old girl suggested the name for "Pluto" after the *Roman god of the Underworld.*

#105 500 seeds of 5 different types were taken into orbit around the moon and brought back. After being planted around the US, as well as in a few other countries, they were called *Moon Trees.*

#106 Sometimes, Pluto is closer to the Sun than Neptune – one of these timelines was from 1979 to 1999.

#107 In space, humans get a little taller because there is no gravity pulling down on them.

#108 In space, the first food eaten by humans was applesauce.

#109 Even in a spaceship, birds cannot live in space because they need gravity to swallow.

#110 On the planet Venus it rains metal.

#111 The rust covering Mars' surface makes the planet appear red.

#112 The moon is very hot. During the day, the temperature can reach 260 degrees Fahrenheit (127 degrees Celsius). But when the sun goes down, temperatures can dip to minus 280°F (minus 173°C).

#113 The sun weighs about 330,000 times more than the earth.

#114 All eight planets in the *Solar System* orbit the sun in the direction of the sun's rotation. Six of them also rotate in this same direction (counter-clockwise). Venus and Uranus are the exceptions, with retrograde rotation.

#115 Even in a spacecraft, a trip to Pluto would take 9-12 years.

#116 It takes light 8 minutes and 19 seconds to travel from the sun to earth.

#117 Footprints on the moon will be there for a million years because there is no wind to erode the surface and no water to wash the prints away.

#118 More stars exist in space than grains of sand are on the world's beaches and deserts.

#119 More than 125 billion galaxies are in our universe. The galaxy we live in has about 100-400 billion stars.

#120 The formation of a *black hole* is caused by the collapse of a large dying star. It has a powerful gravitational force that sucks in everything, including light!

#121 The sun is so big, one million earths could fit inside it!

· 4 ·

FOOD AND BEVERAGES

We, our muscles and our organs, consist of the food and drinks we consume. Our bodies digest what we feed them because that's all it has. No wonder the fast-food eater isn't really that fast, but the one eating healthy foods is filled with energy and motivation to exercise and make things happen.

Our ancestors needed to hunt, collect, and pick berries to survive. Without being active, they weren't able to live. Nowadays, however, it's possible to eat in a restaurant, take your food on the go or even order it at home. This evolution of eating is why we forgot the importance of our nurture. More processed foods, unhealthy beverages and sugary cereals are now on the market and consumed in masses, daily.

Maybe you once learned *"The Food Pyramid,"* but with the forgotten significance of eating, you may have forgotten this useful scheme. If you don't know what it is, I recommend you do some research. The hierarchy represents how much you need of what nutrients; basically, it explains how to eat healthy. Here's a quick list of them, beginning at the top, with the ones you should eat the least: Food and drinks high in fat, sugar, and salt. One level lower: fats, spreads and oils. After that, meat, poultry, fish, eggs, beans and nuts. Followed by milk, yogurt and cheese. Nearly at the bottom, whole-meal cereals, breads, potatoes, pasta and rice. And finally, vegetables, salads and fruits. It needs to be added that water is always the best option to drink.

In my opinion, it's no problem to eat something sweet or some fast-food now and then, as long as it's in moderation. But remember how essential it is to stay healthy and which food and drinks do help you accomplish that.

#122 One bottle of *Coca-Cola* has a pH scale of 2.8, meaning it could dissolve a nail in just four days.

#123 When tea started being sold in bags, initially it was intended to be removed from the bags before brewing. However, customers found it easier to brew the tea still in the bag.

#124 On a genetic level, the fungus is more closely related to animals than to plants.

#125 Cucumber can cure bad breath. If you press a slice to the roof of your mouth for 30 seconds, it allows the phytochemicals to kill the problematic bacteria.

#126 Worldwide, *Subway* has more chains than the fast-food juggernaut *McDonald's*.

#127 Eating a banana can help to prevent heartburn from getting worse.

#128 Carrots have nearly zero fat content and a water content of 86-95%.

#129 Robert Chesebrough, the inventor of *Vaseline*, ate a spoonful of the stuff every single day.

#130 Drink green tea before going to bed. This will burn calories while sleeping. Green tea will also increase your metabolism.

#131 Nearly every brand of hard liquor (bourbon, vodka, whiskey, rum, gin) is vegan.

#132 The inside of a banana skin can polish leather products like handbags or shoes. Simply rub it on and wipe it off with a cloth.

#133 Although several brands claim their soda is older, *Schweppes* is widely considered the most antique one in the world. It was founded in Geneva in 1783. In addition to carbonated mineral water, *Schweppes* sells ginger ale and tonic water.

#134 Many families in Japan eat chicken from *KFC* for Christmas dinner. They order their meals months in advance and queue for hours to collect them.

#135 A natural way to deal with sunburn is by applying non-fat yogurt to a sunburnt area.

#136 Throwing an apple to a woman was considered a symbolic declaration of love in Ancient Greece. And catching it was to show acceptance of that love.

#137 Lettuce is actually a member of the sunflower family.

#138 35,000 hectares (70,000 football fields) of peas are grown in the UK in a single year.

#139 Russians think that eating ice cream will keep you warm.

#140 In Bruges (Belgium) is an underground pipeline that runs 2 miles (3.2 km) to transfer the beer from a brewery to the bottling plant.

#141 In 18th Century England, owning a pineapple was a symbol of wealth because of its high import fees.

#142 When water freezes to ice, it will take up 9% more volume.

#143 About 700 grapes go into one bottle of wine.

#144 In 2016, *Domino*'s started testing pizza delivery via reindeer in Japan. It failed.

#145   *Tic Tacs* got their name from the
sound made when they are tossed
around in their container.

#146   Although there is currently no drug
that has been proven to make someone
tell the truth, some countries like
India, and Russia use *truth serums*.

#147   Try chewing gum when you're writing a
difficult test. It boosts mental proficiency and
is considered a better test aid than caffeine.

#148   During the Second World War, a *US naval
destroyer* won a battle against a *Japanese
submarine* by throwing potatoes at them. The
Japanese thought they were grenades.

#149   Vanilla flavoring is sometimes made
with the urine of beavers.

#150 Almonds are members of the peach family.

#151 If you eat them with your nose plugged, an apple, potato, and onion all taste the same.

#152 Peanuts are one of the ingredients needed to make dynamite.

#153 Cans of diet soda will float in water, and regular soda cans will sink.

#154 Bananas are curved because they grow against gravity and towards the sun.

#155 Baby koalas are fed poop by their parents after they are born, which helps them digest eucalyptus leaves later in life.

#156 Apples float on water!

#157 Tomatoes, cucumbers and avocados are fruits, not vegetables.

· 5 ·

SPORTS AND OTHER ACTIVITIES

"Sport ist Mord" is a German saying, meaning that sports are murder. In some way, it's true because sports can encourage injuries and long-term damage to your body. On the other hand, physical activities are fun (for most people), free the mind, and get your body working.

Sports have been a significant theme throughout human history. In the beginning, they were often used as preparation for hunting or fighting. In 776 BC, the first Olympic Games were held by the Ancient Greeks;

they included activities such as wrestling, races, jumping, and discus throwing. More than 2,000 years later, the Olympic Games are still running and astonishing millions of people all over the world. Championships like this create a stronger bond between the inhabitants of each country and connect the different nations.

But sport doesn't only mean playing soccer or working out. other activities like hiking or going to work on foot will make you a more active person. The human body needs to be challenged, otherwise it will get bored and depressed. If muscles never get used, they will start to regress. That's why it is crucial to participate in some sort of physical activity. Not only will your body know that it's needed, but also will feel awesome after finishing an intensive training.

The same way a workout can exhaust and train your body, it's possible to exercise your brain. This is equally as important, and you are doing it right now. Great job; keep going!

#158 Baseballs had initially been made from the foreskins of horses.

#159 Cricket is the second most popular sport in the world (after soccer/football).

#160 An average golf ball has around 336 dimples.

#161 The UK parliament banned females from participating in dangerous sports.

#162 Olympic gold medals are made of silver.

#163 Actual playing time in a *major league baseball* game is on average less than 18 minutes.

#164 More than 100 million people worldwide have licenses for hunting.

#165 Golf balls were originally made of cow or horsehide and stuffed with feathers, most often goose feathers.

#166 In the ancient *Greek Olympics*, all wrestling matches were in the nude.

#167 At the *2008 Beijing Games*, the Chinese won 100 medals.

#168 The *National Basketball Association (NBA)* was founded on the 6th of June in 1946.

#169 *Extreme ironing* originated in England. It is a sport in which people take ironing boards to remote locations and iron items of clothing.

#170 Alongside chess, Sudoku has been named as one of the best ways to improve the mind and memory.

#171 While walking, you're using a total of 200 muscles with every step you take.

#172 *Gatorade* was invented more than 40 years ago to help the Florida Gators Football Team stay hydrated.

#173 The longest cricket test match, which was held between England and South Africa, lasted over 12 days. It only finished because the English team would have missed their boat home.

#174 Originally, bumper cars weren't supposed to hit each other. Drivers were supposed to avoid crashing despite chaotic driving.

#175 In 1912, the last Olympic gold medals made entirely from gold were awarded.

#176 At the *1908 Olympics* in London, the Russians showed up 12 days late because they used the Julian calendar instead of the Gregorian one.

#177 There exists an underwater version of rugby, unsurprisingly referred to as "underwater rugby."

#178 Did you know that 78% of former NFL players have gone bankrupt or are under financial stress by the time they have been retired for 2 years? This is mostly because of joblessness or divorce.

#179 *Wilt Chamberlain* scored 100 points in one single NBA basketball game (1962). No one has broken this record since then, not even Steph Curry!

#180 The record for the longest jump is held by *Mike Powell*: 29 ft. + 4 inches (8.95 m). That's about like jumping the length of two minivans!

#181 *NFL Super Bowl* referees also get Super Bowl rings.

#182 Cleveland Indians' pitcher *Ray Caldwell* was struck by lightning during a game in 1919. He kept playing!

· 6 ·

SCIENCE AND NUMBERS

To understand how the world works – that's the goal of every scientist, and it has been that way for many, many years before us. Thanks to curious minds like *Thomas Edison* (who invented the light bulb), our world is much more enjoyable than it was hundreds of years ago.

The development of the earth is insane. In 1946, the first computer filled a large room and needed several people to operate. Less than 100 years later, a smartphone as small as a hand and operated by only one finger can do things the first computer couldn't even imagine. But not only technology improved, also biology, chemistry and many more thematic fields were expanded.

For instance, new treatments for the *Ebola disease* have been found. Thanks to improved science, we now know that the virus attacks the immune system and can cause organ failure, resulting in thousands of deaths. In addition to a proven vaccine, researchers have been seeking treatments for patients who already were infected. This is only one example. Countless other discoveries changed the world immensely, like the *periodic table*, the structure of *DNA*, *electromagnetism* and Einstein's *Theory of Relativity*.

The list is endless, and every day, new case studies are conducted. Nevertheless, we are far from understanding everything. That's why we must always seek more education, more knowledge, and more facts.

#183 It is shown that using a hands-free device to talk on the phone while driving is equally or more dangerous than driving drunk.

#184 Daily, 27,000 trees are cut down to supply toilet paper for the world.

#185 When you think of a past event, you remember the last time you remembered it, not the occasion itself.

#186 Giving up alcohol for just one month is very healthy. It improves liver function, decreases blood pressure, and reduces the risk of liver disease and diabetes.

#187 The consumption of sugary drinks is linked to 180,000 deaths per year.

#188 "Cars.com" was the most expensive domain name ever sold. Astonishing fact, that it cost $872.3 million.

#189 While playing offline games on your phone, putting it in airplane mode will stop the ads.

#190 Computers designed for Amish people have selling points like *"No internet, no video, no music."* They really do exist.

#191 Butterflies have an exoskeleton, meaning their skeletons are on the outside of their bodies

#192 In general, people tend to read 10% more slowly from a screen than from paper.

#193 Seven to eight trees are needed to provide enough oxygen for just one person per year.

#194 There is an expansive collection of books under the *British library*'s archive. If a person read 5 books per day, it still would take 80,000 years to complete the whole collection.

#195 Deep snow can sometimes appear blue because the extra layers of snow create a filter for light.

#196 Most customers look at the reviews of a product before they buy it. Reviews help to build trust and can help new readers find a popular book. Why don't you leave a quick review for this book when you finished it :)

#197 The most expensive substance available
in the world is *antimatter*. It costs
about $62.5 trillion per gram.

#198 If you multiply 1,089 by 9, you
get the exact reverse, 9,801.

#199 Roughly 15% of active *Twitter* accounts
are social bots. Meaning there are
nearly 48 million accounts that
are controlled by computers.

#200 The use of tanning beds before age 30
increases your risk of developing *melanoma
(skin cancer)* by 75%. Tanning beds and lamps
are in the highest cancer risk category.

#201 Babies have more bones than adults. As they
grow up, some bones fuse to form one bone.
Newborns have around 305 bones, adults 206.

#202 The *water dropwort* is a highly toxic plant. If it
kills you, it can make you smile after you die.
This smile is called a sardonic grin.

#203 *Volvo* invented the three-point
seatbelt and then gave the
invention away for free. They
decided it was too important
an innovation to keep
to themselves.

#204 Rubber bands last longer when they are refrigerated because it makes the polymers more relaxed.

#205 Any prime number higher than 3, if squared and subtracted by one, will always turn out to be a *multiple of 24*. 5, 7, 11, 13... you can try it out!

#206 The *Star Wars* lightsaber's sound was created by combining the sound of an idle film projector and the hum from an old TV set.

#207 Cranes are built using cranes. But how was the first crane built?

#208 Surgeons who play video games at least 3 hours a week perform 27% faster and make 37% fewer errors during surgery.

#209 Cold showers have more health benefits than warm ones. Advantages include improvement of circulation, stimulating weight loss, and easing depression.

#210 Before Apple bought *Siri*, it was initially going to be released as an app for Android & Blackberry.

#211 Albert Einstein (1879 - 1955) had mastered *calculus* by the tender age of 15.

#212 A study from *Harvard University* found that having no friends can be just as deadly as smoking. Both of them affect levels of a blood-clotting protein.

#213 Amber-colored rear turn signals are statistically proven to reduce collisions by about 28%.

#214 In poker, the odds of getting a *royal flush* are precisely 1 in 649,740.

#215 Gaming-related accidents increased by 26.5% during the first five months of *Pokémon Go* being released. This included two deaths and $25.5 million in damages.

#216 When you shuffle a deck of cards, the number of possible arrangements is *52!* (52 x 51 x 50 x 49 x ... x 3 x 2 x 1). This number is higher than the number of stars in the observable universe.

#217 If you heat a magnet, it will lose its magnetism.

#218 Violin bows are commonly made from horsehair.

#219 Pointing your car keys to your head increases the remote's signal range.

#220 Wearing headphones for just 1 hour could increase the bacteria in your ear by 700 times.

#221 Glass balls can bounce higher than the ones made of rubber (providing they don't break).

#222 A year has 31,556,926 seconds.

#223 There is a 50% chance that in a room with 23 other people, 2 of them will share a birthday.

#224 Number *four* is the only one with the same number of letters as its value.

#225 The opposite sides of the dice always add up to seven.

#226 On average, a yawn lasts 6 seconds, and men yawn longer than women.

#227 The exposure to radioactivity not only affected *Marie Curie* (one of the most famous chemists) but also most of her belongings. Now, more than a century later, her notebooks need to be stored in a lead box, because they are still radioactive (and will be for another 1,500 years)!

· 7 ·

HUMANS

Zoologically viewed, we humans are an upright-walking species called *Homo Sapiens* and developed from primates 315,000 years ago. Our predecessors have always shared the earth with other apelike primates, from long-extinct apes to the modern gorilla. That we are somehow related to apes is accepted by biologists and anthropologists all around the world. But since *Charles Darwin*, a great British naturalist, published his theory, the exact nature of our evolutionary relationships has been the subject of debate. Because the fossil correlation is unclear, experts can't agree on a full chronological series of species, leading to *Homo Sapiens*.

What they can agree on is that as we humans evolved, we started to populate and successfully took over the world. The Ancient Greeks, Romans, Barbarians and more, all created new colonies, spread over the continent, and expanded their empires. It took a long time of exploring, fighting and establishing, until the countries as we now know them were formed.

Nowadays, we don't have to build castles to protect our borders. And it's much easier to focus on our occupations, families and friends. Although our body has transformed through time, the human being has always been a social creature. Only because of the ability to work together, humankind was able to create such an amazing world. Humanity is just incredible!

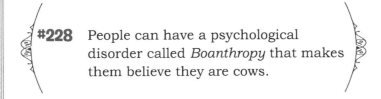

#228 People can have a psychological disorder called *Boanthropy* that makes them believe they are cows.

#229 On average, a person in New Zealand sleeps nearly 7h 45 min per day, making it the "sleepiest country" in the developed world. In Japan, people sleep around 6h 15min.

#230 Using an average of 80 beats per minute, your heart beats about 4,800 times per hour. That's a whopping 115,200 times per day.

#231 The human eye is extremely sensitive. If the earth were flat, and it was night, a candle's flame could be seen from 30 miles (48 km) away.

#232 There are 26 bones in a human foot.

- -

#233 Human beings cannot walk in a straight line without a visual point. When blindfolded, we will gradually walk in a circle.

- -

#234 Remember, next time when your throat tickles, scratching your ear can make it go away.

#235 It is possible to wake up during surgery – how terrifying!

#236 When you see someone you like, the "butterflies" you get in your stomach is a stress response called adrenaline.

#237 The distance from your wrist to your elbow corresponds to the length of your foot.

#238 Ten percent of Filipinos (approximately 10 million people) live outside the Philippines. The country with the highest number of *Overseas Filipinos* is the United States, with 4 million Filipinos.

#239 It takes a red blood cell only about 1 minute to make a complete circuit through your body.

#240 Your immune system can weaken when you are in a negative relationship.

#241 Your brain uses 20% of all oxygen in your body.

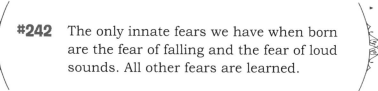

#242 The only innate fears we have when born are the fear of falling and the fear of loud sounds. All other fears are learned.

#243 The tongue is the only muscle in our body that is only attached at one end.

#244 The human eye moves about 50 times every second.

#245 About 25% of all blood coming from the heart goes into the kidneys.

#246 Without saliva, humans aren't able to taste food.

#247 Approximately 1 in 2,000 babies already has a tooth when it is born.

#248 Researchers found that flossing your teeth can help your memory. Flossing prevents gum disease. Gum disease prevents stiff blood vessels, which cause memory issues.

#249 Most people can't lick their elbow. (You can try it!)

#250 If you sneeze too hard, you could fracture your rib.

#251 Like fingerprints, everyone's tongue print is different.

#252 You fart an average of 14 times a day, and each fart travels from your body at 7 mph (11 km/h).

#253 The average person spends 2 weeks of their life waiting at traffic lights.

#254 Before 1913, parents could mail their kids to Grandma's – through the postal service.

#255 A typical cough is 60 mph (96 km/h), a sneeze is often faster than 100 mph (160 km/h).

#256 Sneezing with your eyes open is impossible.

#257 Some people are terrified that a duck is watching them. This is called "Anatidaephobia."

(Update: This word is not officially recognized)

#258 When you look up at a bright sky and see white dots, you are looking at your blood. Those are white blood cells.

#259 The teeth of humans are as strong as shark teeth.

#260 Your nose and ears never stop growing.

#261 About 70% of an adult's body is water.

· 8 ·

LAWS AND RULES

Have you ever seen the film *The Purge*? In this film, one day per year, no rules apply, and nothing is illegal. It is always the most dangerous day of the year, which shows us how important our regulations and laws are. If we want to live in a safe, ordered country, it's crucial to have some guidelines for everyone to follow.

Back when empires had kings, it was their duty to create such rules and punish the ones who didn't obey. The same principles apply today, although, these days the power is distributed among various people, like police officers, judges, and lawyers. All of them act in favor of the security of our nation. In democracies, everyone can vote and come up with new ideas for improvements of the government. There are very few absolute monarchies, where you need to be born into a royal family in order to become the leader.

In the end, I believe the goal of every single person is to live an enjoyable life. And the law is what creates the opportunity for this livable environment. Not only are political rules essential, but at a job or in a sport, the terms also need to be set. Setting such agreements enables us to create fair conditions for each part of a deal. Laws and rules may vary from country to country, and some of them are more useful than others (you will see that in this chapter). But all in all, we need guidelines for living a pleasant lifestyle.

#262 *Kraft Singles* (and other sliced cheese) cannot be advertised as cheese. This is because *US FDA* standards state that food can only be identified as a cheese if it contains "at least 51% real cheese".

#263 It is a federal crime to use the *Netflix* account of your roommate or friend.

#264 In the Northern Territory, Australia, it is illegal to play a musical instrument on a bus.

#265 Northern Korean people are only allowed to have one of 30 haircuts. Men and women must each choose from 15 different styles , each.

#266 According to the *Texas Parks and Wildlife Department*, in Texas it is legal to kill Bigfoot if you find it because it would be considered a non-protected non-game animal.

#267 In New Jersey, it is illegal to wear a bulletproof vest while committing a violent crime.

#268 In India, a law from 1934 classes kites as an aircraft, which is why the flying of a kite is illegal.

#269 In the state of Utah, birds have the right-of-way on a freeway.

#270 In Greece, women are legally not allowed to wear high heels or tall hats in the Olympic Stadium.

#271 China banned the movie "Back to the Future" because it contained time travel.

#272 Even though smoking is prohibited on airplanes, ashtrays are mandatory on every plane. This is meant for safe disposal, in case someone breaks the law.

#273 At *Halden prison* in Norway, guards are encouraged to interact, play sports, and eat with the inmates. This is to help prevent aggression and create a sense of family.

#274 In New Delhi, if a tree gets sick, an ambulance is sent to treat it. This rule came into effect in 2009, and it takes 4 people to do the job.

#275 California law does not prohibit lane splitting. It's the only state in the US that allows motorcycles to pass other vehicles within the same lane.

#276 There are *alien abduction insurance policies*. Around 50,000 of these have been sold, mainly to residents of the US and England.

#277 All new FBI special agents and intelligence analysts have to visit the *United States Holocaust Memorial Museum*.

#278 As specified by the *US Department of Agriculture*, the definition of an original sandwich is "at least 35% cooked meat and not more than 50% bread."

#279 In Los Angeles, 50% of apartments don't come with a fridge. That's legal, as fridges are considered an "amenity," and therefore, landlords are not required to provide one.

#280 There exists a company in the UK that offers "being hungover" as a valid reason for calling in sick to work. They are allocated 4 hungover days per year.

#281 In Mexico, non-violent attempts to escape prisons are not punished because "it's human nature to want freedom."

#282 It's illegal to die in *Svalbard*, a remote Norwegian island.

#283 Only official members of nationwide, recognized Native American tribes may legally possess or collect eagle feathers.

#284 In Uganda, owners of *personalized license plates* face a tax increase of over 300%.

#285 If you cut down a cactus in Arizona, you can be punished by up to 25 years in jail. It is a crime similar to felling a protected tree species.

#286 It's illegal to own just one guinea pig in Switzerland.

#287 When playing in Wimbledon, tennis players are not allowed to swear.

#288   *Facebook*, *Twitter* and *Instagram*
are all banned in China.

#289   In *Sellia* (Italy), dying is illegal. Essentially,
it was meant as a nice gesture,
encouraging people to take care of their
health. But people who do not follow
regular health checks will be fined.

#290   In the streets of London, it's illegal to
beat or shake a mat, carpet, or a rug.

#291   In the United Kingdom, it's an offense
to carry a plank on the sidewalk.

· 9 ·

MONEY

Money doesn't make you happy. This is said everywhere and to everyone. But what about all the things money enables you to do: taking a day off, traveling, buying presents for your loved ones, going out for dinner, and being able to afford a roof over your head. The freedom to do these things definitely helps to make me happy. Of course, it's not healthy to go overboard about money and become a workaholic in order to make as much cash as you can. But it's also extremely stressful to live paycheck to paycheck and have to cut out things you would really like to do.

Overall, money is a fascinating topic. In a nutshell, it's only printed paper or some metal coins with value assigned by society. It all started with *bartering*. That is the exchange of services or resources for a mutual advantage that dates back tens of thousands of years. Then animals, like cows, camels, and sheep, became more popular and were used as a form of money. In 1,000 BC, the first form of metal coins was manufactured by China. And in 118 BC, the first form of banknotes was used—basically, one-foot-square leather pieces with colorful borders.

Nowadays, we are still using notes, except they are made from paper instead of leather. However, the usage of paper money will probably disappear slowly. In our digital age, the future money currency may be electronic. Because most transactions take place electronically now, digital cash will most likely become the currency of the future.

#292 The *US dollar* is the most commonly used currency in the world.

#293 There are 293 ways to make change for a Dollar.

#294 Some countries share a currency. For example, multiple countries in Europe use the *Euro*.

#295 The largest bill ever printed was a $100,000 gold certificate issued in 1934.

#296 *McDonald's* makes about $75 million per day.

#297 Salt was used as a form of money by early Romans — even the word "salary" is derived from *sal*, which means "salt" in Latin.

#298 The world's most expensive object ever built is the *International Space Station* (US $150 billion).

#299 The Icelanders use credit cards and debit cards more frequently than any other country in the world.

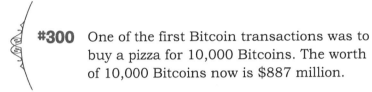

#300 One of the first Bitcoin transactions was to buy a pizza for 10,000 Bitcoins. The worth of 10,000 Bitcoins now is $887 million.

#301 On average, an American family carries a credit card debt of $8,000.

#302 *Apple* earns US $300,000 per minute.

#303 Queen Elizabeth II (born in 1926) holds the record for her image appearing on the most currencies. She is represented on money in at least 35 different countries.

#304 Nowadays, over 170 different currencies are used around the world.

#305 Two-thirds of all printed US $100 bills are held outside the US.

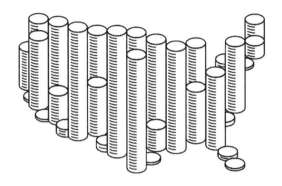

#306 In the world, more than 1.6 million ATMs exist.

#307 Pablo Picasso, who died in 1973, was the wealthiest artist in history.

#308 In 1911, *Mona Lisa* was stolen from the Louvre, which drew more visitors to see the empty space than the actual painting did.

#309 The *British Pound* is the oldest currency in the world, which is still in use (1,200 years old). Its identity is a symbol of British sovereignty.

#310 The total amount spent on adult Halloween costumes each year, in America, is $1.5 billion.

#311 During *World War II*, Germany tried to break down the British economy by dropping millions of counterfeit bills over London.

#312 Money is made in factories called mints.

#313 The first paper money was made in China over 1,000 years ago.

#314 A dime has 118 ridges around the edge.

#315 The *1913 Liberty Head Nickel* is one of the most expensive coins in the world ($4.4 million).

· 10 ·

ANIMAL KINGDOM PART 2

After reading the first chapter, you should already be an expert on this topic. However, I bet you can't remember how many different kinds of animals are living on the earth. To refresh your mind: scientists estimate that around 1 to 2 million diverse species exist. That figure has led experts to guess that the number of individual animals is *20 quintillion*. That's 20 billion billion!

Because of this great number of living animals, there is also a vast amount of facts about them. Besides, everyone loves animals, and that's why we've got a second part with surprising facts about them.

#316 Animals called *stoats* go crazy jumping, spinning, and twisting while hunting so they get a rabbit's attention. This unique technique of hunting hypnotizes the rabbit until the *stoat* gets close enough to attack.

#317 The Guinness World Record for the longest time searching for the *Loch Ness Monster* is held by Steve Feltham. He camped at Loch Ness for 25 years.

#318 If you cut a starfish, it won't bleed because it doesn't have blood!

#319 It is not only humans who are right- or left-handed. Most male cats prefer using their left paw, and females are more likely to be right-pawed.

#320 Sharks living in an active underwater volcano have been discovered by scientists. Divers are not able to investigate because they would get burns from the acidity and heat.

#321 The color *red* doesn't make bulls angry; they are color-blind.

#322 A baby panda right after birth is smaller than a mouse.

#323 The veins of a blue whale are so big a child could swim through them.

#324 Frogs drink water through their skin.

#325 A crocodile cannot stick its tongue out.

- -

#326 Billy goats urinate on their heads to smell more attractive to females.

- -

#327 Elephants stay pregnant for 22 months; it's the longest-lasting period of gestation in any land mammal.

#328 A shrimp has his heart in its head.

#329 Physically, it's impossible for pigs to look up into the sky.

#330 Cat urine glows under black light.

#331 The only fish that can blink with both eyes is the shark.

#332 Cats have 32 muscles in each ear.

#333 An ostrich's brain is smaller than its eye.

#334 Tigers have not only striped fur, but also striped skin.

#335 The giant squid has the biggest eyes in the world (diameter of 10 in / 25 cm).

#336 Rabbits and parrots are able to see behind themselves without even moving their heads!

#337 Butterflies taste food by standing on top of it! Unlike humans who have most taste receptors on their tongue, butterflies have them in their feet.

#338 Although the *Stegosaurus dinosaur* was over 9 meters (30 feet) long, its brain was only the size of a walnut.

#339 Kangaroos and emus struggle to walk backward because of the unusual shape of their legs.

#340 A hippopotamus may seem huge. However, it can run faster than a man. Male hippos can weigh more than 6,000 pounds (2.7 t) and females around 3,000 pounds (1.36 t). Despite their massive bulk, hippos can run up to 30 miles (48 km) per hour!

#341 Snails take the longest-lasting naps, some last as long as 3 years.

#342 Some fish cough. Really.

#343 Goats have rectangular pupils in their eyes.

#344 If a zebra and a donkey have a baby, it is called a *Zonkey*.

#345 Tiger shark embryos begin attacking each other before they are even born. The fight starts when they are still in their mother's womb.

#346 The blue whale is the largest living animal, which can measure as much as 100 feet (30 m).

#347 Nearly 10% of a cat's bones is in its tail.

#348 In the wintertime, reindeer grow their facial hair long enough to cover their mouths, which protects their muzzles when grazing in the snow.

#349 Bamboo makes up 99% of a panda's diet. Sometimes, they eat fish or small animals.

#350 Horses can sleep standing up.

#351 Slugs have four noses.

#352 Owls can't move their eyeballs because they have none.

#353 Hummingbirds, which can beat their wings up to 200 times per second, are the only birds in the world able to fly sideways, backward, up and down. They can even hover in mid-air and fly upside-down.

#354 Male ostriches can roar like lions. And generally, ostriches can run faster than horses.

#355 Usually, a lion in the wild makes no more than 20 kills a year.

#356 You can hear a blue whale's heartbeat from a distance of 2 miles (3.2 km). Its heart is the size of a small car. Naturally, this massive animal would have an equally huge heart. You might miss the heartbeat, though, since it only beats 8 to 10 times per minute.

#357 A kangaroo can't hop if you lift its tail off the ground.

#358 For two days, a swarm of 20,000 bees followed a car because their queen was stuck inside.

#359   Have you ever thought you are forgetful? Don't feel badly. Squirrels forget where they hid about half their nuts.

· 11 ·

RECORDS

Be the strongest, the smartest, the most successful. Everybody wants to be the best. It's that feeling of superiority that makes us think we are something better. But when we reach the top, most of the time, we realize that it doesn't make us happier than before. Look at "successful" people of society. For example, famous music stars often end up in drug addiction and lose everything they worked so hard for. Maybe the sudden fame is too much to handle, and they lose control.

Let's not focus on the negative, but on the extraordinary things that have been accomplished thanks to the drive to become better than everybody else. When looking at sports, some set records seem impossible for a human being; but still, a specific person was able to jump that high or throw that far. Such accomplishments should and definitely do make these athletes proud. Additionally, it can be inspiring for others to become better and work on themselves.

If you think about records, *The Guinness Book of World Records* instantly comes to mind. When looking through this book, we can read about the unbelievable records humans have accomplished. Some performances are simply overwhelming, like one person pulling an airplane or the most blindly-shot free throws in basketball. Others are less incredible and more absurd, like the loudest burp or the longest fingernails. It doesn't matter if you personally want to break that record or not, it's exciting to read about supernatural achievements, anyway!

#360 The largest human mattress domino consisted of 2,019 people (Rio de Janeiro, Brazil, on the 6th of August in 2019). The whole successful record attempt lasted 11 minutes and 13 seconds. After that, all 2,019 mattresses were donated to charities.

#361 *Chad Fell* (USA) set the record for the biggest bubblegum bubble. He blew a bubble with a diameter of 50.8 cm (20 in) without using his hands, on the 24th of April in 2004.

#362 The largest advertising poster measured 28,922.10 m² (311,314 ft²) and was produced for *Arby's* (American fast-food chain) on the 13th of June in 2018. That's four times the size of a soccer field.

#363 The most decimal places of *Pi* memorized is 70,000. It was achieved by *Rajveer Meena* (India) on the 21st of March in 2015.

#364 The widest mouth measures 17 cm (6.69 in). This gigantic mouth belongs to *Francisco Domingo Joaquim* (from Angola).

#365 The highest vehicle mileage is 3,039,122 miles (4,890,992 km). By the 1st of May in 2014, a *1966 Volvo 1800S* had driven this insane number of miles.

#366 The hugest pizza has a total surface area of 1,261.65 m² (13,580.28 ft²). On the 13th of December in 2012, it was prepared by multiple members of *NIPfood* at Fiera Roma, in Rome, Italy.

#367 *Hercules* is the largest living cat. He's an adult male *liger* (lion x tigress hybrid) and currently housed at a wildlife reserve in South Carolina, USA. He measures 3.33 m (131 in), stands 1.25 m (49 in) at the shoulder, and weighs 418.2 kg (922 lb).

#368 *Robert Pershing Wadlow* (born on the 22nd of February in 1918) is the tallest man in medical history for whom there is irrefutable evidence. When he was last measured on the 27th of June in 1940, Robert was 2.72 m (8 ft 11.1 in) tall.

#369 The longest nose of a living person belongs to *Mehmet Özyürek* (Turkey). It measures 8.8 cm (3.46 in) from the bridge to the tip.

#370 *Zeus* (USA) is the tallest dog ever. He's a *Great Dane* who was measured 1.12 m (44 in) high on the 4th of October in 2011.

#371 The longest time that breath was held voluntarily is 24 min 3.45 s. *Aleix Segura Vendrell* (Spain) accomplished this record on the 28th of February in 2016.

#372 The highest mountain in the world is *Mount Everest*. Its peak rises to 8,848 m (29,028 ft) – the highest point in the world. It takes 6-9 weeks to climb it.

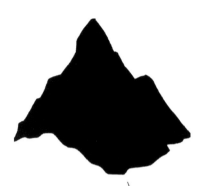

#373 The world longest fingernails belonged to *Lee Redmond* (USA). Lee started to grow them in 1979 and reached a total length of 8.65 m (28 ft 4.5 in). She lost her nails in a car accident in early 2009.

#374 The greatest fully authenticated age to which any human has ever lived is 122 years and 164 days. This record was set by *Jeanne Louise Calment* (France) on the 4th of August in 1997.

#375 *Eminem* holds the world record for the most words in a hit single. "Rap God" packs 1,560 words into a 6 min 4 sec song (on average 4.3 words per second).

#376 *Anna Bagenholm* fell through a frozen stream while she was skiing and was stuck for over an hour. Even though she was clinically dead, she made a full recovery and became the person to survive the lowest body temperature ever recorded (56.7 F / 13.7 C).

#377 In 2005, the largest pumpkin pie ever was baked. It weighed 2,020 pounds (916 kg).

#378 Belgium holds the Guinness world record for the longest time needed to create an official government (589 days).

#379 *Sonic the Hedgehog* holds a record in the Guinness Book of World Records. He is described as the fastest gaming character ever.

#380 One U.S. Park Ranger got hit by lightning seven times and survived all of them.

#381 *Garrett McNamara* holds the record for the biggest wave ever surfed, set in 2011 in Nazare, Portugal. The wave was 78 feet (23.77 m) tall. He had to get towed into the wave by a jet ski.

#382 The highest dying body count in film history goes to *"Lord of the Rings: Return of the King"* with 836 on-screen deaths.

#383 *The Guinness Book of World Records* was started by the manager of *Guinness* when he got annoyed that he couldn't find out which was the fastest game bird ever recorded.

#384 There's a world record for the most world record titles . That belongs to Ashrita Furman, who is from New York. He has set more than 600 official Guinness Records and currently holds 226 records.

#385 The longest wedding veil was longer than 63.5 football fields.

#386 The world record for the most drinking straws stuffed into one's mouth is 459.

· 12 ·

HISTORY AND DATES

For some people, history is a boring topic, an uninteresting subject we were taught in school and for which we had to remember useless dates and numbers. What is *Industrialism*? When did it start? How long did the *Second World War* last? Who was fighting against whom...and so on. But it's important to keep an open mind.

History is more than simply looking backward; it's also critically engaging with the present and learning about the future. To study the past, we don't have to become a professional historian, and anyone who's a curious citizen can do it. When you start engaging with the study of history, you will see that it is much more than learning about kings and governments. It contains the understanding of societies across the world and how they lived over centuries. This teaches us to think analytically, creatively, and to interpret all kinds of information.

But history is even more than that; it is about families, nations, the community. In short, history is about life. These days, huge contemporary challenges of inequality, migration, and climate change require a long-term perspective. By looking at the past and studying the timeless qualities of human behavior, we can make more informed choices about the future.

#387 *Mariner 4* was the very first spacecraft to visit Mars; it was launched in 1964.

#388 The construction of the *Eiffel Tower* started in 1887. Originally, it was planned to be erected in Barcelona, but the project was rejected because citizens thought it was an eyesore.

#389 In 1916, when a producer wanted to enhance the eyes of an actress in a movie, false eyelashes were invented. The lashes were made of human hair.

#390 During WWII, the very first bomb dropped on Berlin killed the only elephant in the *Berlin Zoo*.

#391 One of the first representations of dreadlocks dates from 1500 BC in the *Minoan Civilization*, one of the earliest civilizations in Europe, who lived in what is now known as Greece.

#392 Women have used makeup since before Cleopatra's time. In those days, they used berries and other fruits to give their faces some color.

#393 Back in 1971, *Creeper*, the first computer virus ever, was created.

#394 The earliest mention of the unicorn dates back as far as 2700 BC in Asia. The mythical creature was described as a being of great power and wisdom.

#395 "*Banca Monte Dei Paschi di Siena*" is the world's oldest surviving bank. It was founded in 1472 and is currently Italy's 3rd largest bank.

#396 *Aleksandr A. Serebrov*, a Russian cosmonaut, took his *Game Boy* to space in 1993. It is said to have orbited earth 3,000 times. Later, this legendary *Game Boy* was auctioned for $1,220.

#397 In 1986, because of a bet with the co-pilot, a soviet Aeroflot pilot tried to land the aircraft blindly with all the windows curtained. The plane crashed and killed 70 of the 94 passengers on board.

#398 The *"Pinky Promise"* initially indicated that the person who breaks the promise must cut off their pinky finger.

#399 In 1942, a 12-year-old boy lied about his age and joined the *Navy*. But he was thrown out after his mom found out.

#400 Liège (Belgium) attempted to use 37 cats for delivering mail in the 1870s. Unfortunately, most the cats took up to a day to deliver the post. Therefore, the service was short-lived.

#401 The biggest snowflake in the world was found in 1887. It was 15 inches (38.1 cm) wide and 8 inches (20.3 cm) thick.

#402 The first living creature sent into space was a dog called *Laika* (1957).

#403 It took the radio 38 years to reach a market audience of 50 million people. The television was a little faster with 13 years. But the iPod only took 3 years to get a market audience of 50 million.

#404 A woman was arrested on a beach in Boston (1907) for wearing a one-piece swimsuit.

#405 When *Einstein* died in 1955, his brain went missing and was lost for 23 years. It was stolen and hidden by the doctor who worked on his autopsy.

#406 The oldest present flag of a sovereign state is the Danish flag. It was adopted in 1370 or earlier. The second oldest is the Netherlands' flag, which has existed since 1572.

#407 *Tutankhamun's* parents were cousins. And the pharaoh himself married his half-sister.

#408 The very first roller coaster was used to transport coal down a hill. Some people found out that it could reach speeds up to 50 miles (80 km) per hour. After that, tourists asked to ride on it for a few cents.

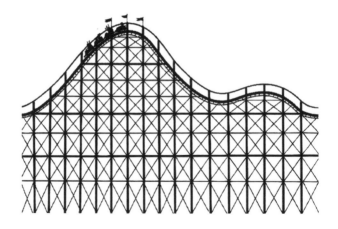

#409   The first designer logo ever was
the famous *Lacoste* crocodile. The
symbol was created in 1933.

#410   *Coca-Cola* was first served in 1886. At that
time, only nine colas were served a day and
3,285 a year. Today, on average, 19,400
Coke products are consumed every second.

#411   *Mickey Mouse* was the first-ever
cartoon character to talk. His first
words, "Hot dogs!" appeared in the
1929 episode, *The Karnival Kid*.

#412   The first jet aircraft was invented in
Germany. The development started in 1936,
but the first takeoff occurred in 1939.

#413   The United Kingdom prints its laws
on vellum, which is made from calf or
goatskin (since 1497). They continue to
do so in order to uphold the tradition
(which is heavily discussed).

#414   The first photograph ever shot, the 1826
photo called *The View from the Window
at Le Gras*, took 8 hours to expose.

#415   In South Korea, on *Valentine's Day*,
only women give gifts, not men.

#416 Plumbers in America call the day after Thanksgiving *"Brown Friday"* because it is their busiest day of the year.

#417 The 29th of May is officially *"Put a Pillow on Your Fridge Day."*

#418 *Doug Engelbart* created the first computer mouse, which was made from wood, in 1964.

#419 In Italy, an entire courthouse was built to prosecute the Mafia. The trial lasted from 1986-1992, and 474 members were charged. To this day, it was the biggest trial in the world.

#420 The 17th of January is known as *"Ditch New Year's Resolution Day."*

#421 In the British Museum, a snail was glued to a specimen card (mid-1800s). After four years fixed there, scientists realized it was still alive.

#422 On the 1st of April in 2005, *NASA* pulled an April Fool's prank telling the world they had found water on Mars.

#423 The odds of being born on the 29ᵗʰ of February are 1 in 1,461.

#424 The 3ʳᵈ of December is known as *"Roof Over Your Head Day"* – a day to be grateful for what we have in life!

#425 The Vatican played music, which was forbidden to be copied. It was a secret for almost 150 years until the 14-year-old *Mozart* heard it and transcribed it from memory.

#426 In 1992, a cargo ship traveling from Hong Kong to the United States accidentally lost a shipping crate in the Pacific Ocean. Nearly 30,000 rubber ducks were lost at sea. Today, they are still being discovered at various beaches.

#427 Soviet Russia built automated lighthouses powered by small nuclear reactors because they needed light on their uninhabited Northern Coast.

#428 In world history, the longest unbroken alliance is between England and Portugal. It has lasted since 1386, and it still stands today.

· 13 ·

LANGUAGE AND LITERATURE

Because of the many different countries and cultures existing in the world, there are also various means of communication and languages. Today, roughly 6,500 languages are spoken on the earth. Sadly, some of them are endangered due to the dynamic communities whose lives are shaped by the rapidly changing world. *Busuu,* for example, is only spoken by 8 people in Cameroon.

Other languages, however, are spoken by huge populations around the globe and are often popular choices among new language learners. Looking at the numbers of total speakers, *English* takes first place with 1,132 million people. However, if we only consider native persons, *Mandarin Chinese* is unbeatable, with its 918 million native speakers.

You've probably heard how challenging it is to learn Mandarin; you need to know around 2,500 (from a total of 50,000) characters to understand 98% of written Chinese. What makes it even harder is that Mandarin is a tonal language, which means that based on the way we pronounce a word, it changes its meaning. One upside is that it doesn't contain tenses, verb conjugations and gender-specific nouns.

English is totally different because of all the tenses and rules that apply. Don't worry, now we're going to look at language and literature from a different perspective, starting with this teaser right now: The word *"goodbye"* was originally an abbreviation of "God be with ye."

#429 *Arctic* and *Antarctic* derive their names to the meanings of "Bears" and "Opposite the Bears."

#430 Malta's official language is *Maltese*. The bulk of the population also speaks English.

#431 The word *"peacock"* doesn't apply to both the male and female birds. Only the males are called *peacocks*, while the females are called *peahens*. The collective name for both of them is *peafowl*.

#432 *Kiss* means "pee" in Swedish.

#433 The letter *Z* is the least frequent letter in written English. It's less common in British English than in American English due to spelling differences, such as "recognize" vs. "recognise."

#434 We all recognize the complexity of the Chinese language. But did you know that the most challenging modern Chinese character requires 23 total strokes to write? This is quán and means "cheek bones."

#435 The word "Android" stands for
a robot with a human appearance.

#436 The band *Led Zeppelin* originally wanted to be
called *"Lead Zeppelin,"* but they felt the "thick
Americans" would pronounce the word wrong.

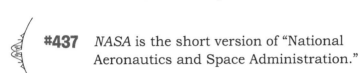

#437 *NASA* is the short version of "National
Aeronautics and Space Administration."

#438 The anxiety of peanut butter
sticking to the roof of your mouth
is called *Arachibutyrophobia*.

#439 *Puma, cougar,* and *mountain lion* are
names for the same animal. The scientific
name is "puma." However, they are more
commonly referred to as "cougars."

#440 Stimulating the salivary glands underneath
your tongue and then spitting a concentrated
jet of pure saliva is called *Gleeking*.

#441 *"Zugzwang"* comes from German and
means when you have to make a choice,
and every option is a bad one.

#442 The origin of the word *"white"*
is from the Indo-European word
"kweit," meaning *to shine*.

#443 *"Musa sapientum"* is the Latin name for *banana*, which translates to "the fruit of the wise men."

#444 Many Greek athletes trained naked for the Olympic games. That's why the word *"Gymnastics"* linguistically means "to train naked." It is derived from two Ancient Greek words: *gumnasía* (athletic training, exercise) and *gumnós* (naked).

#445 The word *"oxymoron"* is itself an oxymoron (two contradictory words appearing together), due to the fact that it derives from Ancient Greek where "oxy" means sharp, and "moros" means stupid.

#446 *"Darth Vader"* is derived from Old Dutch, literally meaning "Dark Father."

#447 *"Schnapsidee"* (English, schnapps-idea) is the German word for a ridiculous idea that only sounds good when you're drunk.

#448 *"Astronaut"* is a compound word derived from two Ancient Greek words: "Astro" meaning *star* and "naut" meaning *sailor*. So astronaut means *Starsailor*.

#449 In Indonesian, there is a word, *"Jayus."* It means "a joke told so poorly and so unfunny that one cannot help but laugh."

#450 The Greeks didn't understand foreign languages and thought it sounded like the other people were saying "bar bar bar" all the time. That's why the word *"barbarian"* originally referred to people who don't speak Greek.

#451 *Twelve* is the largest number in the English language that has just one syllable.

#452 *Bi-weekly* can mean two different things: twice a week, or once every two weeks.

#453 J.K. Rowling got rejected by 12 publishers before the original *Harry Potter* pitch finally was accepted.

#454 The word "almost" is one of the longest in the English language to have all its letters in alphabetical order.

#455 *Eminem's* mother filed an $11 million defamation lawsuit against him (because of his lyrics about her). From the $25,000 she settled for, $23,354.25 of that went to her lawyer.

#456 One *Horsepower* is about 746 Watts. That term was coined in the late 18th century, and one horse can have approximately 15 horsepower.

#457 The terms *"Mr."* and *"Mrs."* originated from using the words *master* and *mistress*.

#458 The English language is not native to the British Isles. Outside invaders displaced Britain's native Celtic speakers and introduced a new West Germanic language.

#459 *Webster's Dictionary* accidentally had a word that didn't exist in it for five years – it appeared as *"dord."*

#460 The only letter which doesn't appear on the periodic table is *"J."*

#461 Even though Irish is the official language in Ireland, Polish is more widely spoken.

#462 *Samsung* means "three stars" in Korean. The founder chose this because he wanted the company to be powerful and everlasting like stars in the sky.

#463 *"IKEA"* is an acronym standing for *Ingvar Kamprad* (the founder's name) *Elmtaryd* (the farm where he grew up) *Agunnaryd* (his hometown).

#464 In English, to leave a party without telling anyone is called a *"French Exit."* In French, it's called a *"partir à l'anglaise,"* which means to leave like the English.

#465 It is believed that *"sixth sick sheik's sixth sheep's sick"* is the toughest tongue twister in the English language.

#466 *"Scraunched"* is the longest one-syllable word in the English language. Two other long, one-syllable words are "screeched" and "strengths," but they only have 9 letters.

#467 *"Dreamt"* is the only English word that ends in the letters "mt."

#468 With 9,690,000 characters *"A la recherche du temps perdu"* (written by Marcel Proust) is the longest book in the world. It tells the author's experiences growing up.

#469 In the English language, there are only 4 words that end in "dous": *tremendous, horrendous, stupendous,* and *hazardous.*

#470 *"Stewardesses"* is the longest word that you only need to use your left hand to type.

#471 *Orange* rhymes with only one word in the dictionary: "Sporadenge." It means a structure in which spores are produced.

· 14 ·

OTHER AMUSEMENTS

The world and everything that comes with it is infinite. You will never know everything, and there's always more to learn and experience. Even if you think you're an expert about a specific topic, you should stay humble and be open to new knowledge and ideas. Keep learning, exploring and researching. That's what makes our life exciting and entertaining.

This book could be huge with the unlimited amount of facts around the world, but who wants to carry around such a big thing? However, your brain is different. It can soak up as much information as you wish without getting any larger or heavier. After a while, it may be difficult to take in any more knowledge because the brain gets exhausted. But the point is that we should be grateful for this gift of a computer-like organ and make good use of it. I encourage you to start (or continue) exploring and not to lose the joy of discovery.

That being said, here come some random facts about other fun stuff.

#472 *Shakira* was rejected from the school choir because her vibrato was too strong. The music teacher in second grade told her she sounded like a goat.

#473 The second-largest purchaser of explosives in the United States is *Disney World* (due to fireworks, etc.). The first being the *US Department of Defense.*

#474 In 2007, a full 1,000-gallon (3,785 liters) inflatable swimming pool was stolen from someone's back yard. A single drop of water was not found!

#475 In Japanese legend, it is said that if you fold 1,000 origami cranes, you will be granted a wish by the gods.

#476 The police in Belfast (Northern Ireland) became creative and used music from an ice-cream van to calm down angry teen rioters.

#477 One in every four cranes on the earth is in Dubai.

#478 It took the Triangle nearly 100 years to become a popular orchestral instrument.

#479 When kissing somebody, around 70% of people tilt their heads to the right rather than the left.

#480 Around 125,000 people get a speeding ticket in the US, every day.

#481 *Albert Einstein* was married to his first cousin, *Elsa Einstein*.

#482 *King Kong* (1933) was the first movie ever to have a sequel.

#483 While filming the Harry Potter movies, *Daniel Radcliffe* broke over 80 wands because he used them as drumsticks!

#484 In Iceland, there's a dating app available that stops you from hooking up with your cousin.

#485 The inflatable pig attached to the power station broke free when *Pink Floyd* designed the "Animals" album cover, causing *Heathrow Airport* to cancel multiple flights.

#486 *Ed Sheeran* (born in 1991) has a ketchup bottle tattooed on his arm.

#487 The word "friends" is said in every single episode of the Friends series.

#488 A customer of a pizzeria "tipped" the waitress $3,000,000 because she helped him choose the numbers for a winning lottery ticket in 1984. The waitress got half of his $6,000,000 prize money.

#489 In Japan, there is a company with schools teaching you how to be funny. The first one opened in 1982. Each year, about 1,000 students take these courses.

#490 *SpongeBob's* voice actor and the voice actor of *Karen* (Plankton's computer wife) have been married since 1995.

#491 In 2005, a 22-year-old man whose name was *Ronald MacDonald* robbed a *Wendy's*.

#492 Some lipsticks contain fish scales.

#493 Eight of the ten biggest statues
in the world are Buddhas.

#494 Bubble wrap was originally invented as
wallpaper. The creators tried to make a
wallpaper out of plastic with a paper backing,
but it came out with plastic
backing.

#495 The Pokémon *Hitmonlee* and
Hitmonchan are based on
Bruce Lee and Jackie Chan.

#496 Elizabeth II, the *Queen
of England,* has two
birthdays. The day of
her actual birth (21st of
April) and one to celebrate with a proper
parade when it's not as cold as in April.

#497 The American President *Lyndon B. Johnson*
(1908 - 1973) owned a water-surfing car.

#498 *Justin Bieber's* very first tweet was at
8:27 pm on the 11th of May, 2009.

#499 Fredric Baur, who was the founder of *Pringles*, requested to be buried in a *Pringles* can in the 1980s. His children honored the request.

#500 Originally, movie trailers were shown after the movie, which is why they were called "trailers."

#501 The oldest "your mom" joke was discovered on a 3,500-year-old Babylonian tablet.

#502 According to director David Fincher, there is a Starbucks coffee cup in every scene of *Fight Club*.

#503 Seven percent of American adults really believe that chocolate milk comes from brown cows. That's more than 16 million American people.

#504 In 2017, more people died from injuries and accidents caused by taking a selfie than by shark attacks.

#505 The 100 folds in a chef's hat represent 100 ways to cook an egg.

#506 The first living passengers in a hot air balloon were a sheep, a duck and a rooster.

#507 If you recycle one glass jar, it saves enough energy to watch television for 3 hours.

Before we head to the next chapter, I would appreciate if you left a review by clicking right <u>here</u> or scanning the QR code below. It only takes 60 seconds to write some short sentences, and this would really help me out. I'm sending greetings to you in advance.

Amazon.com/review/create-review?&asin=B0BMYVZX7F

Quiz

Now it's time to test yourself. How many facts can you remember? How much knowledge have you accumulated? The following quiz shouldn't be perceived as some sort of test or learning control. But you can use it as a refresher of your brain, and it allows you to realize how much you've learned.

Maybe this information will be of great use for you when you're taking part in a TV show, and one of these questions is the key to win. Or maybe you can play this quiz with your friends, and you will be able to look smart next to them.

Every question is on the left-hand side and the associated answer at the right. I advise you to cover the right-hand side with a sheet of paper or something like that. Then uncover the solutions line after line while you're trying to answer the quiz correctly. Or you could invite someone to ask you the questions for even more fun. This way, after you've heard the solution, you might have something interesting to discuss.

These are just suggestions. I don't want to tell you how to handle this book because you should use it how you want and in the way it's most enjoyable for you and everyone else. Have fun!

1) What happens when you keep a goldfish in the dark?

It becomes pale.

2) Which animal can see UV light?

Reindeer.

3) On what special place of the body do bumblebees have hair?

On their eyes.

4) What is the world's largest marsupial?

Kangaroos. They keep growing until they die.

5) What is the world's smallest mammal?

The *Bumblebee Bat*. It weighs about the same as a US dime.

6) Where is the viaduct the *Hogwarts Express* from the Harry Potter movies drove over located?

In Scotland.

7) What percent of the London Underground actually is under the ground?

45%.

8) Where is a town called *Santa Claus*?

In Indiana.

9) How long is the spectacular *Great Wall of China*?

It is 21,196 km (13,170 mi) long.

10) What country does not have a railway system?

Iceland.

11) What was the first soft drink ever consumed in space?

Coca-Cola.

12) On which planet is the tallest mountain in our solar system, *Olympus Mons*?

On Mars.

13) Who suggested the name for Pluto?

An 11-year-old girl.

14) What was the first food eaten by humans in space?

Applesauce.

15) Flying with a spacecraft, how long would a trip to Pluto take?

9-12 years.

16) On a genetic level, is the fungus more closely related to animals or plants?

To animals.

17) What did Robert Chesebrough eat a spoonful of every single day?

Vaseline, which he invented.

18) What is a natural way to deal with sunburn?

Applying non-fat yogurt to a sunburnt area.

19) How many football fields of peas are grown in the UK in a single year?

70,000.

20) In Japan, what animal was tested for doing *Domino's* pizza delivery?

The reindeer.

21) What is the second most popular sport in the world?

Cricket.

22) What are Olympic gold medals made of?

Silver.

23) What were golf balls originally made of?

Cow or horsehide and stuffed with feathers, most often from goose.

24) How many muscles are you using with every step you take?

200.

25) How long did the longest cricket test match last, which was held between England and South Africa?

Over 12 days. It only finished because the English team would have missed their boat home.

26) How many trees are cut down daily to supply the world's toilet paper?

27,000.

27) What was the most expensive domain name that was sold for an astonishing $872.3 million?

Cars.com

28) Why can deep snow appear blue?

Because the extra layers of snow create a filter for light.

29) What happens if you heat a magnet?

It will lose its magnetism.

30) What are the odds that in a room with 23 people, 2 of them will have the same birthday?

There's a 50% chance.

31) What is the "sleepiest country" in the world?

New Zealand. The average Kiwi sleeps nearly 7h 45min per day.

32) How many bones are in a human foot?

26.

33) What will happen if a human being tries to walk in a straight line while having a blindfold on?

The person will gradually walk in a circle.

34) How long does it take a red blood cell to make a complete circuit through your body?

Only about 1 minute.

35) How many times does a human eye move per second?

About 50 times.

36) Are you allowed to use the *Netflix* account of your roommate or friend?

No, sharing a *Netflix* password is a federal crime.

37) How many different haircuts are Northern Korean women allowed to have?

They have to choose from 15 haircuts.

38) What is illegal to wear while committing a violent crime in New Jersey?

A bulletproof vest.

39) In *Halden prison,* guards are encouraged to interact, play sports, and eat with the inmates. Where is it located?

In Norway.

40) Where is it illegal to die?

In *Svalbard,* a remote Norwegian island, and *Sellia* (Italy).

41) When was the first paper money made?

It was made in China, over 1,000 years ago.

42) What is the world's most expensive object ever built?

It's the *International Space Station* (US $150 billion).

43) Who holds the record for appearing on the most currencies?

Queen Elizabeth II (born in 1926), who appears on the currencies of over 35 countries.

44) What is the oldest currency in the world which is still in use?

The British Pound (1,200 years old).

45) How many ways exist to make change for a dollar?

293.

46) Does the color *red* make bulls angry?

No, they are color-blind.

47) How do frogs drink water?

Through their skin.

48) For how long do elephants stay pregnant?

For 22 months.

49) What is the only fish that can blink with both eyes?

The shark.

50) Which animals struggle walking backward because of the shape of their legs?

Kangaroos and emus.

51) For which company was the largest advertising poster, measuring 28,922.10 m² (311,314 ft²), produced?

For *Arby's* (American fast-food chain).

52) How long is the longest nose of a living person?

It measures 8.8 cm (3.46 in) from the bridge to the tip.

53) What is the longest time someone voluntarily held his breath?

24 min 3.45 s.

54) *Eminem* holds the world record for the most words in a hit single. What's the name of the song and how many words does it contain?

The song is called "Rap God" and is packed with 1,560 words.

55) What was the length of the longest wedding veil?

It was longer than 63.5 football fields.

56) Where was the *Eiffel Tower* originally planned to be erected?

In Barcelona.

57) When was *Creeper,* the first computer virus ever, created?

In 1971.

58) Where does the name *"Pinky Promise"* come from?

It initially indicated that the person who breaks the promise must cut off their pinky finger.

59) What was the size of the biggest snowflake, found in 1887?

It was 15 inches (38.1 cm) wide and 8 inches (20.3 cm) thick.

60) How were Tutankhamun's parents related?

They were cousins.

61) What is the least frequent letter in written English?

The letter Z.

62) What does *Kiss* mean in Swedish?

It means "pee."

63) What does *NASA* stand for?

It is the short version of "National Aeronautics and Space Administration."

64) Where do the terms *"Mr."* and *"Mrs."* originate?

From the words *master* and *mistress*.

65) Which word from the dictionary rhymes with *orange*?

Sporange, a structure in which spores are produced.

66) What is the second-largest purchaser of explosives in the United States (after the US Department of Defense)?

It is *Disney World.*

67) How many people get a speeding ticket in the US per day?

Around 125,000.

68) In which country is a dating app available that stops you from hooking up with your cousin?

In Iceland.

69) Why are movie trailers called "trailers?"

Because they were originally shown after the movie.

70) How many American adults believe that chocolate milk comes from brown cows?

7%, that's more than 16 million people.

Conclusion

Finally, after 507 outrageous facts, we end our adventurous journey. I hope you enjoyed reading this exciting information and can make good use of it (more or less). Now you don't have to worry anymore about finding yourself in an awkward moment of silence. You can simply whip out an absurd fact and start making the conversation more fun. Hopefully, you keep your curiosity for learning more, and maybe we'll meet again in the future. As you made it this far, I wish you only the best.

Keep reading to discover even more fun facts & trivia questions. You can skip the Resources section ;)

Resources

40 Interesting Money Facts. (2018, 14th June). Retrieved 23rd June, 2020, from https://www.seriousfacts.com/money-facts/

50 Random Facts that you Won't Believe are True. (2020, 23rd April). Retrieved 25th June, 2020, from https://kidsactivitiesblog.com/76701/50-random-facts/

Animals - mom.me. (n.d.). Retrieved 22nd June, 2020, from https://animals.mom.me/

Arora, M. (2020, 14th January). 50 Spellbinding Science Facts for Kids. Retrieved 18th June, 2020, from https://parenting.firstcry.com/articles/50-spellbinding-science-facts-for-kids/

Bellis, Mary. (2020, 11th February). A Brief History of Sports. Retrieved from https://www.thoughtco.com/history-of-sports-1992447

Bennett, J. (2019, 31st December). The Top Ten Scientific Discoveries of the Decade. Retrieved 19th June, 2020, from https://www.smithsonianmag.com/science-nature/top-ten-scientific-discoveries-decade-180973873/

Cabello, M. A. P. J. S. &. (2019, 6th October). What Japan can teach us about cleanliness. Retrieved 17th June, 2020, from http://www.bbc.com/travel/story/20191006-what-japan-can-teach-us-about-cleanliness

Consumption Of Sugar-Sweetened Drinks Tied To 180,000 Deaths Each Year. (2015, 2nd July). Retrieved 17th June, 2020, from https://www.nwphysicians.com/consumption-of-sugar-sweetened-drinks-tied-to-180000-deaths-each-year/

Daniel, A. (2020, 17th April). 100 Fascinating Facts You'll Want to Share with Everyone You Know. Retrieved 18th June, 2020, from https://bestlifeonline.com/crazy-random-facts/

Eaton, V. (2018, 14th May). 9 Oldest Sodas in the World. Retrieved 22nd June, 2020, from https://www.oldest.org/food/sodas/

ENIAC, World's First Computer. (n.d.). Retrieved 25th June, 2020, from http://www.pimall.com/nais/pivintage/enic.html

Fun Facts for Kids about Sports. (2018, 8th August). Retrieved 21st June, 2020, from https://easyscienceforkids.com/sports-science-fair-projects-facts-for-kids-video/

Guetebier, A. (2020, 4th June). 81 Amazing Facts Every Kid Should Know. Retrieved 18th June, 2020, from https://redtri.com/quirky-facts-and-trivia-for-kids/slide/1

Home. (n.d.). Retrieved 19th June, 2020, from https://www.guinnessworldrecords.com/

How Many Times Does Your Heart Beat in a Lifetime? (2020, 27th February). Retrieved 16th June, 2020, from https://www.wonderopolis.org/wonder/how-many-times-does-your-heart-beat-in-a-lifetime

Maddison -, A. (2019, 7th September). Busuu Blog - language learning tips, inspiration and news. Retrieved 23rd June, 2020, from https://blog.busuu.com/

News: Breaking News, National news, Latest Bollywood News, Sports News, Business News and Political News | Times of India. (n.d.). Retrieved 19th June, 2020, from https://timesofindia.indiatimes.com/

NIEHS Office of Communications and Public Liaison. (n.d.). Kids Environment Kids Health - National Institute of Environmental Health Sciences. Retrieved 20th June, 2020, from https://kids.niehs.nih.gov/games/riddles/jokes/

Nova. (1996, 26th October). The History of Money. Retrieved 18th June, 2020, from https://www.pbs.org/wgbh/nova/article/history-money/

Picard, C. (2019, 27th December). 35 Coolest Random Pieces of Trivia That Will Impress Your Friends. Retrieved 21st June, 2020, from https://www.goodhousekeeping.com/life/g25692093/random-trivia/?slide=2

Say "Prunes," Not "Cheese": The History of Smiling in Photographs. (2012, 4th November). Retrieved 20th June, 2020, from https://petapixel.com/2012/11/04/say-prunes-not-cheese-the-history-of-smiling-in-photographs/

Science Kids. (n.d.). Retrieved 15th June, 2020, from https://www.sciencekids.co.nz/sciencefacts/

Siegel, E. (2019, 20th December). How Many Planets In The Universe? - Starts With A Bang! Retrieved 24th June, 2020, from https://medium.com/starts-with-a-bang/how-many-planets-in-the-universe-9153a05bd0d5

Space.com Staff. (2012, 1st March). How Long Do Footprints Last on the Moon? Retrieved 20th June, 2020, from https://www.space.com/14740-footprints-moon.html

The 25 Most Unbelievable Sports FACTS! - SportsPickle. (2018, 17th May). Retrieved 19th June, 2020, from https://medium.com/sportspickle/the-25-most-unbelievable-sports-facts-41d3d6521679

The Editors of Encyclopaedia Britannica. (2020, 18th May). Pangea | Definition, Map, History, & Facts.

Retrieved 18th June, 2020, from https://www.
britannica.com/place/Pangea

The Fact Site | Fun & Interesting Facts. (2020, 23rd
March). Retrieved 21st June, 2020, from https://
www.thefactsite.com/

Tobin, Declan. (2020). Fun Facts For Kids About
Sports. Easy Science for Kids. Retrieved from
https://easyscienceforkids.com/sports-science-
fair-projects-facts-for-kids-video/

Walsh, G. (2020, 8th June). 37 fantastic facts that
will blow your kids' minds. Retrieved 19th June,
2020, from https://www.goodtoknow.co.uk/
family/facts-for-kids-5446

Wikipedia contributors. (2020, 15th June). China at
the Olympics. Retrieved 18th June, 2020, from
https://en.wikipedia.org/wiki/China_at_the_
Olympics

The Fun Trivia Questions Book

A Small but Mighty General Knowledge Quiz about Random Facts

Zach Olson

Table of Contents

Introduction

Hey, my name is Zach. I love learning new things, and in my opinion, one of the best ways to do so is by doing quizzes. It is a perfect way to discover new facts and also have fun in the process. And that's exactly why I've put together this small book of random but entertaining trivia questions.

While reading or quizzing, you will learn a lot of trivia you didn't know, trivia you never thought about, and trivia you're not sure you want to know. But *The Fun Trivia Questions Book* is more than just a list of questions and answers. For each fact, I give you further background information to tell you the whole story. It is fun for all ages, and you can use it for family game night, when you are on the plane, at the dinner table, at a campfire... just whenever you've got nothing but time.

There are only so many movies to watch, and the trivia inside this book will keep you entertained and fill you up with knowledge. I hope you'll enjoy it!

All Around the World

1. **Where are Albert Einstein's eyeballs?**
   A) In his hometown Ulm, in Germany
   B) In Switzerland
   C) In New York City

In New York City.
The story of Albert Einstein's remains begins shortly after his death in 1955 at Princeton Hospital. There, the hospital's pathologist Thomas Harvey performed an illegal autopsy. Harvey then requested and received a "retroactive blessing" from Einstein's son, Hans Albert, with an understanding that any research conducted would be for scientific purposes. Although Einstein had specific instructions for his remains: "Burn them and secretly disperse the ashes to discourage idolaters," clearly the opposite happened. Harvey preserved Einstein's brain (split it up into anywhere from 170 to over 200 pieces) while also removing his eyeballs. He gave them to Einstein's ophthalmologist Henry Abrams. They are kept in a safe in New York City to this day.

2. **Where does McDonald's serve spaghetti?**
   A) In Russia
   B) In China
   C) In the Philippines

In the Philippines.
McDonald's is known for its classic American fast-food cuisine. Customers love their chicken nuggets, French fries, shakes, and

Big Macs. When you think of McDonald's, these are usually the meals that come to mind. However, in the Philippines, McDonald's also sells the most unexpected dinner: pasta. Yes, McDonald's sells a dish called McSpaghetti. For me, McDonald's and Italian food don't seem like a great mix, but hey–it must be working for some people! According to PopSugar, the McDonald's version of spaghetti is served in a box with the long noodles topped with a generous serving of tomato sauce and shredded cheese. The marinara-like sauce is topped with either ground beef or pieces of sausage that resemble sliced hot dogs. You can even order the McSpaghetti with a fried chicken leg. Sounds delicious, doesn't it?

3. Which famous landmark used to be a lighthouse?
A) The Statue of Liberty
B) The London Bridge
C) The Eiffel Tower

The Statue of Liberty.
Everyone knows the Statue of Liberty as a symbol of the freedom of America, but few are probably aware that many years earlier, it had been an official lighthouse that operated under the supervision of the Lighthouse Board. The burning torch in Lady Liberty's right hand, which still has great symbolic significance, was initially also used as a navigation aid for ships entering New York Harbor. The statue was first lit at 7:35 p.m. on November 1st, 1886, and was put into operation as a lighthouse on November 22nd.

4. Where is the one Starbucks where baristas aren't allowed to write names on the cups?
A) In Las Vegas
B) In the CIA headquarters
C) In the Starbucks Reserve Roastery, Seattle

In the CIA headquarters.
There's only one Starbucks in the world that there's no chance your name will be misspelled on a cup: The one located at the CIA headquarters in Langley, Virginia. No names grace the cups here, much to the frustration of a food service supervisor who complained that things might move faster if they did. And, according to the newspaper, there are tons of people to serve. The place is described as one of the busiest Starbucks in America, with lines that can snake down the hallway.

5. **In which city is it illegal to do "fancy riding" on bikes?**
   A) In Brisbane, Australia
   B) In Glaseburg, Illinois
   C) In Edinburgh, Scotland

In Galesburg, Illinois.
Yes, it's true, you can look it up in the Galesburg Code of Ordinances. It says, "No rider of a bicycle shall remove both hands from the handlebars, or feet from the pedals, or practice any acrobatic or fancy riding on any street." You'd better not try it out!

6. **Where's the shortest railway in the world?**
   A) In Sweden
   B) In England
   C) In Japan

In England.
According to the Guinness Book of Records, the shortest funicular railway is the Fisherman's Walk Cliff Railway in Bournemouth. Built

in 1935, the 128-foot (39-meter) railway has a vertical height of 9 feet (3 meters) and serves millions of people who visit Bournemouth's stunning beaches each year. Taking into account weight, temperature, and wind speed, the journey takes about a minute.

---

7. Does the moon have active volcanoes?

A) Yes, it does

B) No, and it never did

C) No, but it did at one time

No, but it did at one time.

NASA's Lunar Reconnaissance Orbiter (LRO) has provided researchers with strong evidence that the moon's volcanic activity gradually slowed down billions of years ago. Some volcanic deposits are estimated to be 100 million years old, meaning that the moon was ejecting lava when dinosaurs from the Cretaceous period were busy swatting giant dragonflies. There is even evidence of 50-million-year-old volcanism–practically yesterday by lunar standards.

---

8. Were the pubs always open on Saint Patrick's Day in Ireland?

A) Yes

B) No

C) It is not known

No! You couldn't imagine it today, but, until the 1970s, pubs in Ireland were closed on Saint Patrick's Day.

St. Patrick's Day is associated with many things: wearing green, breaking Lent, going to a parade, and of course, drowning the shamrock. There is no other day of the year when the "drunken

Irish" stereotype is more pronounced–and used by some as an excuse to enjoy themselves a bit too much–than on March 17th. In Ireland, this day marks the death of the country's beloved patron saint and has been celebrated as a religious feast day for over a thousand years. This is why, until the 1970s, Irish law banned pubs from opening on March 17th as a sign of respect for this religious day. It was feared that opening the pubs would be too tempting for some during Lent and lead to disrespectful drunkenness on this most solemn day.

9. Which is the only US State capital without a single McDonald's?

A) Juneau, Alaska

B) Montpelier, Vermont

C) Santa Fe, New Mexico

Montpelier, Vermont.

When traveling to a big city in the US (or most other countries), it seems like there is a McDonald's on every street corner. But not in Montpelier, the state capital of Vermont. To be fair, it's not as glaring an omission as it might seem. Montpelier is the smallest state capital, in terms of population, with only around 7,500 inhabitants. It also prefers local businesses over large chains, so McDonald's should not take this personally. The city doesn't have a Burger King, either.

10. What percentage of the Sahara Desert is sandy?

A) approximately 25 percent

B) approximately 55 percent

C) approximately 95 percent

Approximately 25 percent.
The Sahara is the largest hot desert in the world. It is located in North Africa and covers large parts of the continent: 3,320,000 square miles (8,600,000 square kilometers), which is comparable to the size of China or the USA. Sand dunes only cover about 25 percent of the actual surface of the Sahara. The desert also has numerous other land features, including salt flats, gravel plains, plateaus, and even mountains where snow has been recorded.

11. Where is the only Shell gas station that is shaped like a shell?

A) In Bournemouth, England

B) In Winston-Salem, North Carolina

C) In Tucson, Arizona

In Winston-Salem, North Carolina.
There were once eight shell-shaped gas stations in North Carolina: seven in Winston-Salem and one in nearby Kernersville. These Shell Oil gas stations were built in the 1930s by a local distributor of Shell Oil and were intended to serve as hard-to-miss advertisements to entice customers to drop by. Wouldn't you choose to get your gas from a fun place like this over an old, boring, normal gas station? Today, only one of these Shell stations is left. The final remaining clamshell station is on the corner of East Sprague and Peachtree Streets in Winston-Salem. You can still stop at the glorious yellow-stuccoed street attraction to take photos, but don't show up with an empty tank: It's no longer a working gas station! The station closed in the 1950s and briefly housed a lawnmower store in the 1970s and 1980s. But today, the shell is only for show. Just because the old Shell gas station lost its function doesn't mean this North Carolina roadside attraction will disappear soon—it was added to the National Register of Historic Places in 1976.

12. What colors do passports around the world come in?
A) Black, red, yellow, and blue
B) Black, red, white, and blue
C) Black, red, green, and blue

Black, red, green, and blue.
Passports are only made in four colors: black, blue, red, and green. Surprisingly, there are no official rules or regulations governing what colors passports have to be. Countries are free to choose any color they want, and there are many variations in the shades of blue, black, green, and red used for passports. But why are passports available in these colors? Probably, because they look the most official. The dark colors also hide signs of dirt and wear and tear. Countries choose them because they look more official than, for example, neon pink. The color that a country chooses can be determined by both culture and historical significance. For example, the color green has a religious meaning for Islamic countries. Burgundy–a shade of red–is the preferred color for countries in the European Union, while India has a blue passport. However, there are certain rules that all countries must follow: passports should be made of a material that can bend, won't wrinkle, and can withstand chemicals, extreme temperatures, humidity, and light.

13. Where is the world's largest national park located?
A) In Russia
B) In Canada
C) In Greenland

In Greenland.
With an area of 375,000 square miles (972,000 square kilometers),

the Greenland National Park is the largest in the world. The area is almost the size of France and Spain combined and includes the entire northeastern part of Greenland. The coast is 11,000 miles (18,000 kilometers) long and includes both the highest parts of the largest ice cap in the northern hemisphere and the northernmost area of land. Various Inuit cultures have lived and survived here for thousands of years, thanks to the high number of Arctic species.

14. Where are shadows darker, on the Earth or on the moon?

A) On the Earth
B) On the moon
C) They are equally dark

On the moon.
On Earth, the movement of living things, the changes in the natural and cultural environments, and the weather which traps the sunlight to varying degrees make the shadows very dynamic. Air scatters light and allows objects not exposed to direct sunlight to be well lit. This is an effect called Rayleigh scattering, named after the British Nobel Prize winner Lord Rayleigh (John William Strutt). Rayleigh scattering is why the skies are blue and why you can still read a magazine perfectly well under an umbrella on the beach. However, as there is no air on the moon, there is no Rayleigh scattering. So shadows are very dark and it is very bright where sunlight comes in. Areas of shadow are dramatically cloudy, but some light is still reflected in them–this is due to reflected light from the lunar surface itself.

15. How long did it take to build the Eiffel Tower?

A) 1 years, 3 months, and 7 days
B) 2 years, 2 months, and 5 days
C) 3 years, 1 month, and 4 days

2 years, 2 months, and 5 days.
On June 12th, 1886, the decision was made to build the iron tower proposed by Gustave Eiffel during the competition for the Exposition Universelle, which was to be opened on May 15th, 1889. That only left him 3 years to build the tower. Additionally, it took another 6 months to obtain the country's concession from the city of Paris for negotiations with the state. Work began in January 1887 with the construction of sixteen masonry foundation blocks, one per edge. The foundations were completed 6 months later, and assembly of the metal structure began in July 1887. There were less than 2 years left to build the tower, but they managed to finish it on time. The secret of this rapid assembly was the complete prefabrication of the tower's 12,000 parts in Eiffel's workshops in Levallois-Perret, which had already begun during the construction of the foundations. There, all the parts were calculated, drawn, cut, drilled, and pre-assembled with rivets, then sent to the construction site and returned to the workshop in the case of defects. Two-thirds of the tower's 2,500,000 or so rivets were set in the factory. Modest steam cranes and between 150 and 300 well-supervised workers were enough to assemble all the prefabricated metal parts in 22 months. What a masterfully executed project!

16. Where is the largest waterfall in the world?
A) In the USA
B) In Canada
C) In the ocean

In the ocean. More specifically, in the ocean between Greenland and Iceland.
Rivers that flow over the gorges of the Earth form waterfalls that are natural wonders and attract millions of visitors due to their breathtaking beauty, size, and power. But no waterfall is larger or more powerful than those that lie beneath the ocean (yes beneath!) and cascade over immense cataracts hidden from our view. In fact, the world's largest waterfall lies beneath the Strait of Denmark, which separates Iceland and Greenland. At the lower

end of the strait is a series of cataracts that start 2,000 feet (600 meters) below the surface of the strait and descend to a depth of 10,000 feet (3 kilometers) on the southern tip of Greenland– nearly a two-mile drop. But how can there be waterfalls in the ocean? This is because cold water is denser than warm water and, in the Strait from Denmark, southward-flowing frigid water from the Nordic Seas meets warmer water from the Irminger Sea. The cold, dense water quickly sinks below the warmer water and flows over the giant drops of the ocean floor, creating a downward flow.

17. Where did a woman call the police because her ice cream didn't have enough sprinkles?
A) In Denmark
B) In the USA
C) In England

In England.
West Midlands Police in England released a record of a woman calling the emergency number to help in an argument about sprinkles on her ice cream. She contacted the police after arguing with the owner of an ice cream truck. During the minute-long call, she said to the emergency services: "It doesn't seem like a major emergency, but it is a little bit because I ordered an ice cream, and he's put bits on one side but none on the other. He refuses to give me my money back and says I have to take it like that." Chief Superintendent Jim Andronov warned against abusing the emergency system. If someone is trying to report a real life-or-death emergency, one minute is a very long wait. He added that about 50 percent of calls to the 999 operators are not emergency calls. For example, in another case, a caller wanted to seek help after forgetting his Facebook password!

18. Why is there no airport in the country Andorra?

A) Because the country is too small

B) Because there are too many mountains

C) Because there are not enough inhabitants

Because there are too many mountains.
Airports have become symbols of economic and social progress. As a means of transport, it has advantages that others simply cannot offer. The speed, distance, and connections that airplanes and airports offer are second to none. This is why it is so rare to find a country without an airport. But there are some, for example, Andorra. The Principality of Andorra is not as small as you might think. Its surface area is 180 square miles (468 square kilometers), so there's room for several airports, but the problem here is the mountains. The co-principality lies between Spain and France and is isolated from the rest of Europe by the Pyrenees that completely surround it, peaks that are nearly 10,000 feet (3,000 meters) high. At such altitudes, modern aviation is difficult and dangerous, especially when fog or ice is added to the equation. And that's why the Andorra-La Seu d'Urgell Airport is located in Spain, 10.8 miles (17.4 kilometers) from the border with Andorra.

Science and Crazy Numbers

19. What's the highest denomination note ever printed?
A) The $10,000 gold certificate bill
B) The $100,000 gold certificate bill
C) The $100,000,000 gold certificate bill

The $100,000 gold certificate bill.
The $100,000 bill with the portrait of President Woodrow Wilson was actually a gold certificate that was never circulated or issued for public use. The Bureau of Engraving and Printing produced it in 1934 during the Great Depression to conduct official transactions between Federal Reserve banks. Only 42,000 of the $100,000 bills were ever printed. While the $100,000 bill cannot be legally kept by collectors, some institutions such as the Museum of American Finance issue them for educational purposes. The Smithsonian Museum and some branches of the Federal Reserve System (FRS) also hold these rare bills. Their value today is estimated at about $1.6 million.

20. What's the normal operating engine temperature of a car?
A) Between 90 and 104 degrees Celsius (195 and 220 degrees Fahrenheit)
B) Between 85 and 99 degrees Celsius (185 and 210 degrees Fahrenheit)
C) Between 79 and 93 degrees Celsius (175 and 200 degrees Fahrenheit)

Between 90 and 104 degrees Celsius (195 and 220 degrees Fahrenheit).

Most modern vehicles have a display that shows a constant temperature value of the coolant circulating in the engine in order to give the driver an early warning of a problem in the cooling system. For most automobiles, the normal engine temperature is in the range of 90 to 104 degrees Celsius (195 to 220 degrees Fahrenheit). On average, the temperature needle is at or near the center when the engine is at normal operating temperature, which usually takes at least a minute or two to reach after starting a cold engine. Using the air conditioning at full power, stop-and-go driving on a scorching day, and towing may raise the engine temperature above normal. Don't panic if the display changes slightly. You can pull off the street for a while or turn off the air conditioning and turn on the heater to cool things down. Yes, you read correctly; turning on the heater will cool down the engine.

21. Who invented a car controlled by a joystick?
A) Ferrari
B) Mercedes
C) Ford

Mercedes.

As the name suggests, the "Mercedes F200 Imagination" was not only a visionary and innovative proposal from Mercedes-Benz but also an extremely ambitious project. Its most important feature is the future-oriented dynamic handling system "Drive-by-Wire" with which the driver could control the entire vehicle movement with a joystick. Steering was done by moving the joystick in the desired direction; pushing the control stick forward accelerated the vehicle, and pulling back applied the brakes. The steering wheel and pedals are removed, which means that the passengers have more space and, therefore, more comfort.

22. What household appliance inspired one of the first pairs of Nikes?

A) A refrigerator
B) A toaster
C) A waffle iron

A waffle iron.

The co-founder of Nike, Bill Bowerman, who was a legendary track and field coach at the University of Oregon, made the white waffle spike shoes for one of his runners at the school. They were made in the early 1970s and modified in 1974 to add the "waffle sole," a major innovation in Nike history. Bowerman invented the design after taking inspiration from his wife's waffle maker. He partnered with former Oregon runner Phil Knight in 1964 to create Blue Ribbon Sports. In 1971, the two renamed their business Nike and started a company that would eventually dominate the global sportswear market. In 2019, the legendary waffle sneakers were auctioned at an astonishing $475,500.

23. Which building grows more than 6 inches (15 centimeters) during the summer?

A) The Burj Khalifa Tower
B) The Eiffel Tower
C) The Leaning Tower of Pisa

The Eiffel Tower.

Until 1930, the Eiffel Tower was the tallest building in the world. Named after its founder Gustave Eiffel, it was intended to set an example for the French Revolution and function as a radio transmission tower. The Eiffel Tower gets up to 6 inches (15 centimeters) higher in summer when the temperature reaches 40 degrees Celsius (104 degrees Fahrenheit). Extreme heat expands the metal at the base and increases the height of the 1,000-foot (320-meter) tower.

24. At what temperature do tennis balls need to be stored for the Wimbledon tournament?
A) At 18 degrees Celsius (64 degrees Fahrenheit)
B) At 20 degrees Celsius (68 degrees Fahrenheit)
C) At 22 degrees Celsius (71 degrees Fahrenheit)

At 20 degrees Celsius (68 degrees Fahrenheit).
During each tournament at Wimbledon, 54,250 balls are used. They are swapped out every seven to nine games. Because of the effect of temperature on the ball performance, all balls are stored at 20 degrees Celsius (68 degrees Fahrenheit), and each one is tested for bounce and weight. Inside a tennis ball is a hollow core that contains gas. If the temperature of the ball changes, the pressure of the gas inside changes, which influences the ball's physical dynamics.

25. Which is the biggest single-celled organism?
A) Caulera faxifolia
B) Caulerpa taxifolia
C) Caulepa taxifoli

Caulerpa taxifolia.
Caulerpa taxifolia is a green algae and species of seaweed that can become up to 12 inches (30 centimeters) long. It is considered to be the largest single-celled organism in the world. Its surface is enhanced by a frond-like structure, and it is coenocytic, which means that it's a single cell with multiple nuclei. This makes it like a multicellular organism but without the division between cells.

26. How can new equipment for the Space Station be up there within seconds?

A) Thanks to extremely fast rockets
B) Thanks to teleportation
C) Thanks to 3D print technology

Thanks to 3D print technology.

It used to take months or even years to get new equipment to the space station, depending on the replenishment schedule. Nowadays, tools can be printed out in the space station. Many of the specifications for the equipment were preprogrammed into the 3D printer before it left Earth, while others are sent as files from Earth into space. Sending a file to the station is as quick as sending an email. The technology opens up opportunities to create objects that could not even be brought into space before.

27. How long is the shortest passenger flight in the world?

A) 90 seconds
B) 120 seconds
C) 180 seconds

90 seconds.

It could very well take longer to read this story than flying on the world's shortest scheduled flight. Loganair, a Scottish regional airline, holds this title thanks to its route between Westray and Papa Westray, two of the Orkney Islands north of Great Britain. The cost of a one-way ticket starts at £17 (about $22) and the flight, which travels 1.7 miles (2.7 kilometers), takes only 1.5 minutes in the air. This seems like nothing compared to the 19-hour flight of the Australian airline Qantas. The 10,200-mile (16,200-kilometer) non-stop trip from New York to Sydney is the longest flight in the world.

28. Does bleach expire?

A) Yes

B) No

C) I don't know

Yes, after about 1 year.

Bleach is very effective at killing germs and viruses and disinfecting all types of surfaces at home. However, it is only effective if it has not expired. The bleach actually begins to degrade or break down about six months after the date of manufacture. After six months, the concentration of bleach is lower than when it was first made, but it can be effectively used for disinfecting for up to a year. When bleach degrades, it breaks down into water, salt, and oxygen. Hence, it is not effective for sanitizing anymore.

29. Which organization tests its product's durability with a butt-shaped robot?

A) IKEA

B) Samsung ·

C) Tommy Hilfiger

Samsung.

Deep inside Samsung's headquarters in Suwon, South Korea, countless employees spend most of the day putting the company's latest cell phones through a series of grueling, wincing durability tests. Before a Samsung smartphone can hit the market, the electronics giant wants to make sure that it can withstand a significant beating and continue to function properly.

Fun with Words

> **30. Which came first: Orange the color or orange the fruit?**
>
> A) Orange the color
> B) Orange the fruit
> C) This is not known

Orange the fruit.

The citrus fruit got named orange first. The word for the fruit originated from old French, and the first time it was recorded in English dates back to the 1300s. The word's use as the name of a color appears in the early 1500s, 200 years later. As oranges were widely available on the market, people started to also use the word for the color. Before then, English speakers referred to the color orange as "yellow-red."

> **31. What does the clothes store H&M stand for?**
>
> A) Haus & Mode
> B) Her & Him
> C) Hennes & Mauritz

Hennes & Mauritz.

The origins of this Swedish brand go back to the 1940s, according to the H&M website. It was in 1947 when Erling Persson, a Swedish entrepreneur, opened a women's clothing store. This store, located in Sweden, was called Hennes, which means "Hers" in English. In 1968, Hennes decided to buy "Mauritz Widforss," a retailer of hunting and fishing clothing and equipment.

Unfortunately, there's no fancy Swedish meaning for Mauritz other than the name of the man who originally started the brand.

32. Was the dunce cap always a visual symbol of idiocy and punishment?
A) Yes
B) No
C) What's a dunce cap?

No–let me explain.

Nowadays, few people refer to dunce caps anymore. The caps themselves were usually made from rolling paper into a cone and writing a "D" or the word dunce/fool on the paper to indicate to viewers that the person wearing the cap had done something remarkably stupid. It is known as a dunce cap, dunce's cap, dunce hat, or dunce's hat. But, it turns out that the origin of the fool cap is filled with irony. The dunce cap was once viewed as something closer to a wizard's hat. While we understand today that the goofy-looking cone hat signified some kind of intellectual failure, it actually began as a symbol of respected scholars.

33. Where does the abbreviation Xmas come from?
A) From the Greek
B) From the Hebrew
C) From the Roman

From the Greek.

The history of the word Christmas is actually more fascinating than you might think. First of all, the abbreviation is way older (centuries) than its use in bright advertisements. It was first used in the mid-16th century. X stands for the Greek letter "Chi," the first letter of the word "Χριστός" (Chrīstos), which means Jesus

Christ. That's why X has been an acceptable representation of the word Christ for hundreds of years which therefore led to the word Xmas.

34. What do you call a flock of ravens?
A) An unkindness
B) An ominousness
C) An airsickness

An unkindness.
There is speculation about the origin of the term. Some suggest that it goes back to the creature's symbolic association with witches and death. Others refer to the ravens' "kleptomaniac habits" when it comes to other birds' eggs. In light of recent findings, however, the collective name could be seen as unkind in itself. Scientists at the Institute for Research on Wildlife Resources (IREC) found that ravens have a significantly lower impact on the population growth of their prey than other predators. Whether this means they are unfairly maligned is a matter of opinion, but one thing is certain: These winged creatures are highly intelligent and possess strong social skills. They are able to recognize the dynamics within a group, even if they have never belonged to it. The only other creatures known to be capable of this are humans.

35. Which letter does not appear in any US state name?
A) The letter J
B) The letter Q
C) The letter Z

The letter Q.
Only one letter? Yes, only Q isn't contained in any US state name.

Every other letter of the alphabet appears at least once. Fifty different names and not one of them contains the letter Q. I bet many of you guessed J, X, or Z, as these letters also seem very rare. And you're right, they are. But if you said they don't appear in any state name, you probably don't live in New Jersey, Texas, or Arizona.

36. What is a cow-bison hybrid called?

A) A "Bicow"

B) A "Beefalo"

C) A "Buffcattle"

A "Beefalo."
There are many benefits to crossing a cow with a bison. USDA testing showed that beefalo possess superior vitamin levels, higher protein, less cholesterol, 79 percent less fat, and 66 percent fewer calories than conventional beef. Also, beefalo cuts have received the "Best Steak" award at the American Royal Steak Competition for several years in a row. And last but not least, it is famous for being a healthier beef for you and the world.

37. How many words and expressions for snow exist in Scotland?

A) 251

B) 379

C) 421

421.
Academics have officially registered 421 snow-terms that Scots use—including "skelf" (a large snowflake), "sneesl" (to begin to snow), "snaw" (snow), and more. Researchers propose that this variety of terms originated from the ancestors of the Scottish

people. It shows the importance for them to communicate about the weather which could easily affect their livelihood. Here are some more cool expressions: "feefle" (to swirl), "flindrikin" (a slight snow shower), "snaw-pouther" (fine driving snow), "spitters" (small drops or flakes of wind-driven rain or snow), and "unbrak" (the beginning of a thaw).

38. What is the unique ant species in New York called?
A) TimesSquareAnts
B) ManhattAnts
C) YorkAnts

They are called ManhattAnts.
The residents of Manhattan are arguably a breed all their own. The same goes for their ants. Especially somewhere between 63rd and 76th Streets, where biologists have discovered a completely new species of ant. "It's new to North America, and we believe it's new to the whole world," said Rob Dunn, the professor of biology whose team discovered the insect. The Big Apple insects were tentatively named "ManhattAnts" until a more scientific nomenclature could be arranged. It's a relative of the cornfield ant, and it looks like it originated in Europe.

39. What was the last letter added to the alphabet? And no, it's not Z.
A) J
B) Q
C) Y

It's J.
It's no coincidence that I and J are next to each other in the

alphabet–they were considered the same character for centuries! The letter J began as a swing letter, a typographic embellishment for the pre-existing I, which was used to mark the end of a series of ones–as in "Henry viij" for Henry the 8th. Both I and J were used interchangeably to express the sound of both the vowel and the consonant until the Renaissance grammarian Gian Giorgio Trissino argued for the independence of the poor letter J in 1524. After being snubbed for nearly three centuries, J was finally recognized as a full-fledged letter in the 19th century, making it the baby of the English alphabet.

40. Where does the word "OK" come from?
A) from the words "all correct"
B) from the words "oh key"
C) from the words "alright clear"

It comes from the words "all correct."
We say it and type it countless times a day, but have you ever thought about what "OK" actually stands for? And is it right to write "OK" or is it "okay"? People know what the word means–it's a verbal thumbs-up to indicate approval–but for most of us, where this unique expression comes from is a mystery. If you go through the trouble of typing two extra characters to spell "okay," you're technically wrong. It's more correct to write "OK" because it's actually an acronym from the 19th century. OK stands for "oll correct" or "all correct." Back then, it was part of a trend for writers to playfully misspell and abbreviate their words, just for fun. They were even more creative with abbreviations than they are today, LOL.

41. What is an anagram for Albert Einstein?
A) Ten elite brains
B) The elite brain
C) Elite brain test

Ten elite brains.

It seems incredibly appropriate that the genius Albert Einstein's name is an anagram of the phrase "ten elite brains." Meaning that the exact same letters are used for his name and the phrase but differently arranged. It is also an anagram for "elite brain nest" and "brainliest teen." Coincidence?

Food and Drinks Trivia

42. How old is the oldest wine?

A) At least 1,000 years old

B) At least 1,350 years old

C) At least 1,650 years old

At least 1,650 years old.

Wine has a long and rich history in human existence that predates even written records. One theory postulates that the fermentation of alcohol took off between 10,000 and 8,000 BC. But, unfortunately, we don't have bottles from that early era anymore. The oldest bottle of wine, known as "Römerwein" or "The Speyer Wine Bottle," is at least 1,650 years old. This goes back to the 4th century, sometime between 325 and 359 AD. The 1.5-liter glass vessel was discovered during the excavation of a Roman aristocratic grave in modern-day Germany. If you're wondering how this old wine smells or even tastes–we don't know. Experts are uncertain what would happen to the liquid if it were exposed to air. So it has remained sealed with its thick stopper made of wax and olive oil since then.

43. What are the different flavors of "Froot Loops?"

A) lime, orange, grape, lemon, cherry, and strawberry

B) lime, orange, grape, lemon, cherry, and raspberry

C) There are no different flavors

There are no different flavors, they all taste the same.

I hate to tell you this, but you've been eating a bowl of lies for breakfast the whole time. It turns out that the delicious, multicolored Os that make up Froot Loops don't represent different fruit flavors. Kellogg's says that all of these delicious loops are flavored the same. If you fell into your cereal bowl after reading this, you are not alone. We have all been misled by these tantalizing lime green, orange, purple, yellow, and red loops as if they tasted of lime, orange, grape, lemon, cherry, and strawberry when in fact, they all have the same flavor. People at FoodBeast did some scientific blind testing and found the rumors to be true: Froot Loops all taste the same. They found that blind taste tests of "Trix" and "Fruity Pebbles" produced similar results.

44. When was the first espresso drunk in space?
A) In July 2010
B) In April 2012
C) In May 2015

In May 2015.
Italian astronaut Samantha Cristoforetti had the pleasure of tasting the first espresso brewed in space thanks to a pioneering coffee machine designed to operate in space. The aerospace engineers developed a new concept of coffee machine that is safe for astronauts and can function in microgravity conditions. This capsule-based coffee machine was created with the collaboration of Italian coffee maker "Lavazza," "Argotec" (an Italian engineering company that specializes in the design of aerospace systems), and the Italian Space Agency (ISA). The machine, which takes its name from the International Space Station, is called "ISSpresso" and can also create a variety of other hot drinks.

45. Are strawberries botanically seen as berries?
A) Yes
B) No
C) How should I know?

No, they're not.
Strawberries and raspberries are not actually berries in the botanical sense. They derive from a single flower with more than one ovary and are therefore an aggregate fruit. True berries are simple fruits that come from a flower with one ovary and typically have multiple seeds. Tomatoes fall into this group, as do pomegranates, kiwis, and, believe it or not, bananas. (Their seeds are so small it's easy to forget they're there.) So bananas are berries, and raspberries are not. Now you know.

46. How old are supermarket apples?
A) They are approximately 1 week old
B) They are around 1 month old
C) They can be up to 1 year old

They can be up to 1 year old.
In the USA, apples are harvested from August to November. Apples that will sell through December are regularly refrigerated. These huge warehouses are kept at 1-3 degrees Celsius (34-38 degrees Fahrenheit). Apples that will be sold later go to controlled atmosphere storage. They are stored at lower temperatures and oxygen levels. The oxygen level is reduced to 2 percent (the normal oxygen level is 21 percent). Sounds like they won't be as good anymore, but if handled and stored properly, the apples will taste just as when they went in. Apples lose some acidity when stored, but the nutritional content does not change significantly. This is why they can be sold for many months after harvesting.

47. What fruit glows blue under black light?
A) The kiwi
B) The banana
C) The orange

The banana.
The usual appearance of bananas is mainly due to carotenoids. These natural pigments appear yellow in normal light and blue under UV light (known to party guests as black light). However, green, unripe bananas do not fluoresce because the intensity of the luminescence correlates with the breakdown of the green pigment chlorophyll. Researchers in Austria were surprised to find that the intensity of the blue light peaks at the point where the fruit is perfect for eating. What an invention that would be: ripe bananas as the nightclub's new eatable glow sticks!

48. Have you ever eaten wasabi?
   A) Yes
   B) No
   C) Maybe

Probably you think yes, but maybe you have not, because most wasabi paste isn't real wasabi.
90 percent of the time that people eat "wasabi," they are actually eating dyed green horseradish. Now that we know we've been living our lives next to imposter wasabi, sharing our table and nasal passages with a fraud, let's get into how that could happen. Actual wasabi is extremely rare and extremely expensive; 2.2 pounds (1 kilogram) of wasabi can cost up to $250. One of the few places where wasabi grows naturally is in Japanese mountain streams. Wasabi plants require very special conditions in order to grow and thrive: constant flowing spring water, shade, rocky soil, and temperatures between 7 and 20 degrees Celsius (46 to 68 degrees Fahrenheit) year-round. So, wasabi is hard to grow, which makes it rare, which makes it expensive, which means you were probably eating green horseradish, and you didn't know until now.

49. What special beverage equipment is furnished in British battle tanks?
A) Juice press equipment
B) Beverage cooling equipment
C) Tea-making equipment

Tea-making equipment.
Few things are more British than tea, although it was originally a Portuguese tradition to brew South Asian leaves. The culture of tea drinking permeates British society–including the military. However, the culture of the tea break has been a major issue for the generals in charge of Britain's armored formations. Tank crew members had to stop and get out of their vehicle to have a brew, making it difficult to maintain an armored advance safely. The answer was the British Army boiling vessel: a built-in boiler for armored vehicles.

50. Why was the tomato feared in Europe in the late 1700s?
A) Because Europeans thought it looked dangerous
B) Because Europeans thought it was poisonous
C) Because Europeans thought it tasted bad

Because Europeans thought it was poisonous.
A nickname for the fruit was the "poison apple" because it was believed that aristocrats got sick and died after eating it. But the truth was that wealthy Europeans used pewter plates that were high in lead to serve the tomatoes. Because tomatoes have such a high acidity, when placed on this particular dish, the fruit would leach lead from the plate. This would lead to many deaths from lead poisoning. At the time, nobody made that connection between plate and poison, so the tomato was selected as the culprit.

51. Why was PEZ candy invented?

A) To help people quit smoking
B) To help people quit eating meat
C) To help people quit chewing gum

To help people quit smoking.
I think we all know PEZ, not for its especially good flavor but for the cool dispensers with their plastic head. PEZ, an abbreviation for "Pfefferminz," which is German and means peppermint, was invented in Austria in 1927 by Edward Haas. Haas developed a mint that he wanted to market as an alternative to smoking. In this way, Haas was way ahead of its time; cigarettes weren't considered bad back then. Although there's no evidence that peppermint is useful to stop smoking, the campaign proved to be quite successful in Austria. Probably because of the candy's sugar, which is now known as an effective drug addiction substitute, rather than the taste itself.

52. Which fast-food giant once made bubblegum-flavored broccoli?

A) McDonald's
B) Subway
C) Pizza Hut

McDonald's.
It sounds like one of Willy Wonka's rejected ideas, but this one is for real. Don Thompson, the chief executive of McDonald's, tried to create a way to get kids to eat healthier. This idea arose from the pressure of not having enough healthy options on the menu. Unfortunately, adding sweet bubblegum flavor to broccoli didn't make it more appetizing to children–they were more confused by it. Let's hope Willy Wonka will come up with a better idea!

53. What animal once put a man in the hospital because a shot bounced off it?
A) A turtle
B) An armadillo
C) A nautilus

An Armadillo.

A Texan man who tried to shoot an armadillo landed in the hospital after his bullet bounced off the animal and hit him in the face. The police said the man spotted the little animal "on his property" around 3:00 a.m. local time and decided to kill it. He went outside with his revolver and shot the armadillo three times. Its hard shell deflected at least one of the bullets, which bounced off and hit the man's jaw. That's karma!

54. How can flamingos balance on one leg while sleeping?
A) They have an excellent sense of balance
B) They have balance aids built into their bodies
C) They don't sleep with all parts of the brain at the same time

They have balance aids built into their bodies.

The fantastic balance flamingos have has something to do with their anatomy, especially a built-in "hold mechanism." The bird's skeleton seems to be the key. As in humans, flamingos have two main joints on their legs. The one you can see bending backward is not the knee. This is actually the bird's ankle. Its knee is hidden in the bird's features in the thicker part of its body. When the flamingo is ready to nod off, it will lift one leg and instinctively move its body so that its single foot is centered just below its carriage. Meanwhile, pulling up the other leg forces the knee on which the flamingo rests to bend. All of the joints essentially snap into place. Since the flamingo stays almost completely calm while sleeping, gravity does the rest and keeps the bird in place.

55. How do lobsters taste their food?
A) With their nose
B) With their legs
C) With their antennas

With their legs.

The four small antennas on the front of the lobsters' heads are used to "smell" their food or chemicals in the water. Smell operates over distances, but taste requires physical contact. That's where the tiny sensory hairs on their legs come into play. They are used to "taste" their food. When the lobster smells food, it then crawls around until one of its legs brushes the food to get a taste of it.

56. How do sea cucumbers fight?
A) They puff up to appear more dangerous
B) They hide very fast
C) They fight with their guts

They fight with their guts (literally).

The defenseless-looking sea cucumber has a secret weapon. When attacked, it spits sticky threads from its anus, tangling the hunter. Sea cucumbers can expel all of their intestines from their anus. This can confuse, repel, or feed predators. As extreme as this defense sounds, a cucumber can regenerate its internal organs quickly and without dying.

57. Can bees make colored honey?
A) Yes
B) No
C) It is not known

Yes, when they don't collect nectar from flowers.
Beekeepers in northeastern France found themselves in a difficult situation when their bees began producing honey in shades of blue and green from their hives. The honey was not allowed to be sold because it did not conform to French standards for honey production. Instead of collecting nectar from flowers, bees on site were feeding on leftover colored M&M candy shells that were being processed at a biogas plant about 2.5 miles (4 kilometers) away. The waste-processing plant discovered the problem at the same time as the beekeepers and quickly cleaned up all outdoor or uncovered containers where M&M waste had been stored. The candy residue is now stored in a covered shed.

58. How heavy is a blue whale's tongue?
A) It can weigh as much as an elephant
B) It can weigh as much as a horse
C) It can weigh as much as a pig

It can weigh as much as an elephant.
The blue whale dives to a depth of 330 feet (100 meters) to eat millions of krill a day and receives the award for the largest creature. These blue-gray giants are 80 to 100 feet (24 to 30 meters) long and weigh about 400,000 pounds (180,000 kilograms). This is equivalent to the weight of 135 cars. Its tongue alone weighs 5,400 pounds (2,400 kilograms), and a blue whale's

heart is about the size of a VW Beetle. Blue whales are quite large from birth and are considered to be the largest babies in the world. According to the World Wildlife Fund, a blue whale calf is about 26 feet (8 meters) long and weighs about 8,000 pounds (3,600 kilograms).

59. Who can hold their breath longer: sloths or dolphins?
A) Sloths
B) Dolphins
C) They can hold their breath for the same length of time

Sloths-they can hold their breath four times longer than dolphins.

Sloths are one of the most magical creatures in the world. They are adorable, love warm climates, laze around all day, and their furry bodies are home to hundreds of other organisms. But these lovable mammals have a lot more to offer than you might think. Sloths can swim three times faster in the water than they walk on land. And due to their ability to slow their heart rate to a third of its normal rate, they can hold their breath for 40 minutes, even underwater! On average, dolphins can hold their breath for a total of 8 to 10 minutes. They adjust their bodies as necessary to maximize their diving and catching fish time. Although Dolphins can slow the blood flow and heart rate of their circulatory system to conserve the energy and oxygen needed to stay underwater, sloths can hold their breath four times longer.

60. How big is the world's smallest wasp?
A) It is smaller than an ant
B) It is smaller than a grain of sand
C) It is smaller than an amoeba

It is smaller than an amoeba.
Fairies do exist and can be found in your garden. But you'd need a powerful microscope to see the dainty creatures. Fairy wasps are tiny parasitoid wasps with feather wings. Often, they are called fairy flies, which is a misnomer because they aren't actually a species of flies. Found in the United States, they belong to the Mymaridae family, which includes the smallest known insects in the world. Most species are less than 0.04 inches (1 millimeter) long–smaller than the average pinhead. And the smallest of all is a wingless male specimen of the fairy wasp at about 0.005 inches (0.13 millimeters). Many species of insects are sexually dimorphic, which means that males and females can look so different that they can be mistaken for different species. For the fairy wasp, the females are much larger than the record-breaking tiny males.

61. When do South American river turtles begin to communicate with one another?
A) When they are still in their eggs
B) When they are hatching
C) When they are in the ocean

When they are still in their eggs.
When it comes to saying their first "words," South American giant tortoises are amazingly precocious. Researchers discovered that the baby turtles begin to talk up to three days before hatching. Probably, the turtles communicate to coordinate hatching, which occurs 45 to 50 days after the eggs are laid. That offers security in numbers from predators. So when the turtles start to migrate, they'll call the other turtles and say "let's go, let's go, it's time."

62. Which animal washes its food before eating?
A) Wild boars
B) Elephants
C) Foxes

Wild boars.

Multiple animals submerge or manipulate their food in water prior to consumption. But not all of these animals actually have the intention of washing it. Some species of birds simply moisten their food to make it easier to swallow. Raccoons often roll it around in the water, but the behavior reflects their constant need to use their hands to sense the world and forage–not the urge to wash their food. To confirm that an animal really aims to remove dirt and sand from its food, researchers needed to see that it can distinguish between clean and dirty food and that it is deliberately moving dirty food to a water source. The discovery that some pigs wash their food came by accident. The communications officer at Basel Zoo in Switzerland noticed that wild boars put sandy apple halves in their mouths and carried them to the edge of a creek that ran through their habitat, put the pieces of fruit into the water, and manipulated them with their snouts before eating.

63. Is it okay to give your cat milk?
A) Yes, it's no problem
B) No, you shouldn't do it
C) Cat's love it, so why not?

No, you shouldn't do it.

In children's stories, cats and milk always seem made for each other. Who hasn't seen adorable illustrations of a kitten licking a saucer of cream? Most cats do love a little milk, but milk doesn't always return that affection. The main culprit is lactose which many cats have trouble digesting. Just like humans, cats can be lactose intolerant. In order to digest lactose, a milk sugar, the human and feline digestive systems must contain the enzyme lactase. At birth, we have plenty of this enzyme in our bodies, and it helps us live off our mother's milk. But as we grow up, it's normal for humans and cats to produce less lactase. Less lactase means less ability to digest lactose. The result: diarrhea or an upset stomach.

64. How many hearts does an octopus have?
A) 1
B) 2
C) 3

Octopuses have 3 hearts.
1 pumps blood around the body, and the other 2 pump blood into the gills. The reason for this impressive heart hardware is likely due to the unusual composition of their blood. In contrast to vertebrates, which have iron-rich hemoglobin in red blood cells, octopuses have copper-rich hemocyanin dissolved right in their blood (funny side note: this makes their blood blue!). Because hemocyanin is less effective as an oxygen transporter, the three hearts are needed to compensate for this by pumping blood around the body at higher pressures.

65. Which animals have the most neck bones?
A) Sloths and manatees
B) Giraffes and lamas
C) Ostriches and flamingos

Sloths and manatees.
Really? Is it not the giraffe? Nope. As a rule, all mammals have the same number of vertebrae in their neck, regardless of whether they are a giraffe, mouse, elephant, or human. But both sloths and

manatees are exceptions to this rule, with ten vertebrae instead of seven. It is believed that it's their slow lifestyle and low metabolic rate that have allowed evolution to change their neck lengths.

66. How high could a bumblebee fly?

A) Higher than the highest roller coaster

B) Higher than the highest building in the world

C) Higher than Mount Everest

Higher than Mount Everest.

Scientists have found that alpine bumblebees have the ability to fly at elevations greater than Mount Everest, but they cannot survive the freezing conditions at its peak. Researchers at the University of California simulated the conditions of low oxygen and air density at such high elevations to determine the limits of the bumblebee's flight capacity and found that the bees would be able to stay afloat at remarkably inhospitable elevations.

67. Which animal was used by Ancient Egyptians to ease toothaches?

A) The mouse

B) The cat

C) The dog

The mouse.

The ancient Egyptians put a dead mouse in their mouth in the hope that it would relieve toothache. In some cases, mashed mice were mixed with other ingredients, and the resulting poultice was applied to the painful area. The Egyptians weren't the only ones engaged in mouse cures. In Elizabethan England, one remedy for warts was to cut a mouse in half and apply it to the affected area. Mice were also used to treat whooping cough, measles, smallpox, and bed-wetting. To top it all off, the Elizabethans also ate mice—fried or baked in cakes. Eww!

68. Why can't cows really bite you?
A) Because they don't have front teeth
B) Because they don't have lower front teeth
C) Because they don't have upper front teeth

Because they don't have upper front teeth.
Cows are unique in that they have fewer teeth than other animals. In the front of the mouth, they have teeth only on the bottom jaw. Instead of the upper teeth, there is a hard leather pad. Because of this unique oral anatomy, a cow reaches for a tuft of grass with its tongue and "bites" it off. But in the back of the mouth, teeth are located on the upper and lower jaw, which they use for chewing the grass.

69. Which animal lay 56,000 eggs at a time?
A) The turtle
B) The octopus
C) The crocodile

The octopus.
A pregnant squid carries the eggs in her body for 4 to 5 months. One day, when the water temperature is right, she begins to expel her eggs into the water, one by one. She produces about 56,000 individual eggs, which takes about a month. Later, after some more months of guarding the eggs, the female octopus dies when their babies descend into the ocean. Out of these 56,000 eggs, sadly, only about two of them make it to adulthood.

70. How long are giraffe tongues?

    A) Up to 16 inches (40 centimeters)

    B) Up to 18 inches (45 centimeters)

    C) Up to 20 inches (50 centimeters)

They are up to 20 inches (50 centimeters) long.

Much like their necks, giraffe tongues are exceptionally long–usually between 18 and 20 inches (45 to 50 centimeters) long. They're also prehensile, which means that giraffes have fine-tuned muscular control over them. This allows them to grab leaves and shoots and pull them into their mouths. The dark purple color of the tongue is supposed to prevent sunburn. This may sound strange at first, but it makes sense considering that giraffes spend most of their day sticking their tongues out to retrieve grass shoots and leaves.

71. How many calories do blue whales eat in one mouthful?

    A) One quarter million calories

    B) Half a million calories

    C) One million calories

Half a million calories.

The average person consumes 2,000 calories a day. Doesn't sound like a lot compared to the blue whale, eh? Scientists in Canada estimated that a blue whale can eat 480 million calories of food in a single dive (which lasts about 10 to 20 minutes). In one day, these whales consume around 12,500 pounds of food to fuel their body! 8 months a year feeding occurs, and then the whales live on their blubber reserves for the other 4 months.

Humorous History

72. What was the tiny pocket in jeans designed for?

A) To look high-end

B) To hide keys

C) To store pocket watches

To store pocket watches.

Those little pockets are far too small to be useful. But in the olden days, they were designed to hold a pocket watch. They are not usually found on suit pants because suit jackets already have pockets for watches. These days, people tend to check the time on their cell phones or watches, so pretty much no one carries around a pocket watch. However, the small pockets are kept in jeans today to maintain the integrity of the original design.

73. How long did the shortest war in history last?

A) 18 minutes

B) 28 minutes

C) 38 minutes

It lasted 38 minutes.

On August 27th, 1896, five Royal Navy ships began bombing the Royal Palace and Harem in Zanzibar. 38 minutes later, the bombardment stopped as the white flag of surrender was raised over the remains of the palace. Over 500 defenders died compared to one injured British Marine. This ended what is known as the "shortest war in history." The immediate cause of the war was the death of the Sultan of Zanzibar, Hamad bin Thuwaini, on August 25th. His nephew took power but was seen by the British as far too independent. In the best tradition of gunboat diplomacy, an ultimatum was issued, giving Khalid an hour to surrender and leave the palace. When the ultimatum expired, the bombardment began. The nephew was quickly and secretly shipped out of the country. Order was restored, and the preferred ruler, Hamud bin Muhammed, was installed as Sultan of Zanzibar, where he ruled with British support until his death in 1902.

74. When was the first female elected to Congress in the United States?
A) In 1916
B) In 1936
C) In 1956

In 1916, even before women had the right to vote nationally. Jeannette Rankin of Montana was the first woman elected to Congress. Rankin had campaigned as a progressive in 1916, pledging to work for a change in constitutional women's suffrage and to emphasize social welfare issues. She was a committed pacifist for a long time and against US involvement in the European war that had been raging for two years.

In 1917, she arrived at the Capitol to be sworn in with the other members of the 65th Congress (1917–1919). When her name was mentioned, the house cheered and rose so that she had to rise and bow twice, which she did in complete self-possession.

75. What did Americans use before toilet paper?
A) Leather
B) Corn cobs
C) Their clothes

Corn cobs.

Anyone who's gone camping will know that a handful of dry leaves comes in handy when there's no toilet paper around. Modern toilet paper wasn't available in the United States until the mid-19th century. Before it was made in the ubiquitous four-and-a-half-inch rolls we all know and love, toilet paper came in bundles of flat sheets about the size of a box of today's facial tissues. But before that time, native Americans used twigs, dry grass, small stones, and even oyster or clamshells. In rural farming communities, handfuls of straw were often used, but one of the most popular means of cleaning was dried corn cobs. They were plentiful and very efficient at cleaning–they could be drawn in one direction or rotated around an axis. They were also softer in sensitive areas than you might think. Even after toilet paper became available, some people in western states preferred corn cobs when using the outhouse.

76. When does the first urine-based pregnancy test date back to?
  A) It dates back to 450 BC.
  B) It dates back to 850 BC.
  C) It dates back to 1,350 BC.

It dates back to 1,350 BC.

One of the earliest written records of a urine-based pregnancy test is found in an ancient Egyptian document. One papyrus described a test in which a pregnant woman could urinate on wheat and barley seeds for several days: If the barley grows, it means she'll have a male child; if the wheat grows, a female one. And if neither grows, she won't bear at all. Tests of this theory in 1963 found that 70 percent of the time, the urine of pregnant women promoted growth, while the urine of non-pregnant women and men did not. Scientists have identified this as possibly the first test to detect a unique substance in the urine of pregnant women and have speculated that elevated levels of estrogen in the urine of pregnant women may have been the key to success.

77. Why were roller coasters invented?

A) To make people more content

B) To distract people from immoral behavior

C) To show off the latest inventions

To distract people from immoral behavior.

Riding roller coasters is one of the most popular pastimes in the world. People sometimes wait for hours to ride the newest thrill ride or an old classic. There are many reasons why we enjoy riding roller coasters: People love the speed, the apparent danger, and like a small child riding a wagon a little too fast on a winding side path, we like to be scared. Oddly enough, none of these things was the main reason behind the invention of the roller coaster. What motivated the inventor of the roller coaster at the end of the 19th century was immorality. Believing that America had both created and rushed into a cave of iniquity, LaMarcus Adna Thompson was looking for a pastime that would pull Americans away from the tavernas, game and dance halls, and brothels. Thompson was inspired by people riding an old mining railway for fun and built his own "Switchback Railway." In three weeks, Thompson was making about $600 a day–that's the equivalent of $15,000 a day today! It didn't take long until others started to develop their own switchback railways.

78. How long did the first commercial passenger flight last?

A) 13 minutes

B) 23 minutes

C) 33 minutes

It lasted only 23 minutes.

In 1914, on January 1st, the world's first scheduled airline took off between St. Petersburg and Tampa, Florida. The St. Petersburg-Tampa Airboat Line was short-lived, but it paved the way for today's daily transcontinental flights. Abram C. Pheil, former mayor of St. Petersburg, was the first paying passenger. The 21-mile (34-kilometer) flight across the bay to Tampa took 23 minutes. Pheil paid $400 (more than $8,500 in today's dollars) but considering the alternative transport options, it may have been worth it. A trip between the two cities on opposite sides of Tampa Bay took up to 12 hours by train. The drive through the bay by car took about 20 hours.

79. Where did baseball umpires use to be during a game?

A) They used to be sitting in a rocking chair
B) They used to be sitting in a spectator seat
C) They used to be sitting on the ground

They used to be sitting in a rocking chair.
Baseball has been around for over one hundred years, and in the early days, umpires would officiate games reclining in a rocking chair positioned 20 feet behind home plate. Imagine seeing this in today's game on national television! In 1878, the National League also declared that home teams had to pay umpires $5 per game.

80. What was the biggest empire in history?

A) The Roman Empire
B) The Greek Empire
C) The British Empire

The British Empire.
The British Empire began with colonies and trading posts overseas and ended up including dominions, protectorates, and mandates. It covered 13.01 million square miles (33.6 million square kilometers) of land–more than 22 percent of the Earth's landmass. In 1938, the empire had 458 million people–more than 20 percent

of the world's population. The financial burden of World War I was the beginning of the end for the British Empire. Finally, Japan's occupation of its territories in World War II and the loss of India in 1947 ended the glorious days of the British Empire.

81. What did paint used to be stored in?
A) In pig bladders
B) In horse stomaches
C) In cow intestines

In pig bladders.
John G. Rand, a brilliant but little-known American portrait painter, struggled to keep his oil paints from drying out before he could use them. At that time (1841), a pig's bladder sealed with string was the best paint storage device. The artist poked the bladder with a pencil to extract the paint. But there was no way to completely seal the hole afterward, and the bladders did not transport well and often burst. But Ran came up with a revolutionary invention: the paint tube. This foldable pewter tube, sealed with a screw cap, made the paint last a long time, did not leak, and could be opened and closed again and again.

82. When was the first official aquarium opened?
A) In 1853
B) In 1913
C) In 1963

In 1853.
The earliest documented aquarists were the Sumerians, who kept freshwater fish in man-made ponds at least 4,500 years ago, and records of fish keeping also date from ancient Egypt. However, only in 1853, the Zoological Society of London opened the first

modern public aquarium, displaying over 300 marine species in closed tanks called the "Fish House." The term aquarium (which comes from classical Latin: a watering place for cattle) was coined by the British naturalist Philip Henry Gosse and shortly thereafter adopted and popularized by the London Zoo. 8 years later, in 1938, the first oceanarium (large saltwater aquarium), Marineland, opened in Florida.

83. Who invented glitter?
A) A New Jersey cattle rancher
B) A New Jersey beekeeper
C) A New Jersey teacher

A New Jersey cattle rancher.
You might not have expected it, but glitter has actually been used as a decoration since prehistoric times. Cave paintings were discovered with mica flakes mixed in to give them a shimmering appearance. The word "glitter" itself comes from the Old Norse word "glitra" and means "shine," but modern glitter as we know it today was not invented until 1934. The inventor, Henry Ruschmann, tried to figure out a way to dispose of plastic. He shredded it and accidentally fabricated glitter.

Famous and Not-So-Famous People

84. Who is the man with the world's deepest voice?
A) Tim Thunders
B) Tim Hurricane
C) Tim Storms

Tim Storms.
The hearing range of most mammals is wider than the range of frequencies they can produce with their voices. For example, the human ear can hear frequencies up to 20 kHz, but we cannot scream higher than approximately 3 kHz. The lower end of our listening range is around 20 Hz. This is still just below the lowest notes most of us normally make, which is around 85 Hz. US singer Tim Storms, however, can sing a note at 0.189 Hz, or eight octaves below the lowest G note on the piano. Crazy!

85. What did Michelangelo write on the ceiling of the Sistine Chapel?
A) A poem about how he didn't like painting the chapel
B) A poem about how he enjoyed painting the chapel
C) A poem about how grateful he was for painting the chapel

A poem about how he didn't like painting the chapel.
Michelangelo, one of the best-known artists in history, didn't always enjoy his (art) work. As a gifted poet, sculptor and painter,

he wrote energetically about desperation and described with relish the unpleasant side of his work on the famous ceiling. The poem conveys that the Italian artist knew well enough that he and his work were great but that he enjoyed violently lamenting his discomfort, pain, and inadequacy for the job. "My painting is dead" or "I am not at the right place–I'm not a painter" are parts of the poem that demonstrate his despair due to the hard time working on this challenging project.

86. Who scored the winning goal in the first World Cup?
A) The one-legged Héctor Castro
B) The one-armed Héctor Castro
C) The one-footed Héctor Castro

The one-armed Héctor Castro.
Although today's highly professional world of football may at first glance seem like a zone of no disability, when we look back on the first World Cup tournament in 1930, Héctor Castro, a one-armed man, played an extremely important role. In the 89th minute, he scored the sixth and final goal of Uruguay's 4–2 win in the 1930 playoff. Castro had lost half an arm in an accident with an electric saw thirteen years earlier and, despite this amputated limb, won Olympic gold and scored the first and, above all, last goal in Uruguay.

87. Does Queen Elizabeth II have a secret double?
A) Yes
B) No
C) We don't know, it's a secret

Not, but she has a "stand-in" for rehearsals.
Technically, the Queen does not have a body double. There is currently no person attending engagements in place of the queen. However, Ella Slack has played an important behind-the-scenes role as a "stand-in" for the Queen over the past three decades. Ella Slack insists that she is not a lookalike. "I don't look like the Queen–but I have the same stature and size," she explains. Ms. Slack's job is to help promoters, stage managers, and production staff figure out exactly how the Queen will fit into important events.

It all started when she was at the BBC when the Queen stood on the Cenotaph, and there was sunshine in her eyes. Since the stage managers were all six-foot-tall men, Ms. Slack stood in the Queen's place so they could adjust the lighting. This first substitute role led to other assignments, including driving the Queen's royal carriage and attending the rehearsal for the opening of Parliament. Of course, since Mrs. Slack is not the Queen, she still has to follow certain protocols. She is never allowed to sit on the throne in the House of Lords but must lurk above it. This is a very strict rule. However, Ms. Slack is allowed to give the iconic royal wave in the Queen's carriage. And who doesn't want to do that?!

88. Which former US President was shot right after giving away his good-luck charm?
A) Abraham Lincoln
B) William McKinley
C) Theodore Roosevelt

William McKinley.
William McKinley is one of the few presidents that have been assassinated, but his assassination has a very special twist. McKinley had worn a lucky red carnation on his lapel for years, but one day he decided to give it to a little girl at the Pan American Exhibition in Buffalo, New York. Moments later, he was shot, which apparently shows that lucky charms are very real, at least in his case.

89. Who tries to fix the internet?

A) Its creator

B) Its shareholders

C) Nobody

Its creator, Tim Berners-Lee.

The inventor of the World Wide Web officially launched his plan to "fix" the Internet. The World Wide Web Foundation, a nonprofit campaign group, founded by Berners-Lee, has won the support of technology giants Facebook, Google, and Microsoft for what is known as the "Contract for the Web" program. The treaty calls on companies to respect consumer privacy and urges governments to ensure that everyone has access to the internet. "Never before has the web's power for good been more under threat," said Adrian Lovett, CEO of the World Wide Web Foundation. He added that the rise of hateful content and fake news spread online means that something has to change. They are planning to launch the world's first global action plan to protect the Internet as a driving force. It will bring together businesses, governments, and citizens from around the world to get things back on track.

90. What do Mahatma Gandhi, Eleanor Roosevelt, and Adolf Hitler have in common?

A) They have all been Nobel Peace Prize nominees

B) They have all been assassinated

C) They have all been born less than 150 years ago

They have all been Nobel Peace Prize nominees.

Yes, Adolf Hitler, the genocidal mastermind of the Shoah, was nominated to the Nobel Committee in 1939, just three months before he led Germany to invade Poland and start World War II. The recommendation came from a Social Democratic member of the Swedish Parliament, Erik Gottfrid Christian Brandt. (Members of national assemblies are among the many people who can nominate candidates for the Peace Prize.) In his letter to the committee, he calls the Führer "a God-given fighter for peace" and "the Prince of Peace on Earth." He calls *Mein Kampf* "the best and most popular piece of literature in the world" and is confident that the dictator can "pacify Europe and possibly the whole world." Sound like sarcasm? It definitely was. Brandt was an anti-fascist and had described the letter as ironic. Later in 1939, after the war broke out, he wrote that he had wanted to use the letter's sarcasm to "nail Hitler to the wall of shame" as enemy number one of world peace. Angered by the prestigious award, which had been given to his critic Carl von Ossietzky in 1935, Hitler had banned all Germans from accepting the prize.

91. Why is the British royal family named Windsor?

A) They're named after the fashion brand Windsor
B) They're named after the House of Windsor
C) They're named after the town of Windsor

They're named after the House of Windsor, which was founded in 1917.

Before 1917, the British royal family members did not bear a surname but only the name of the house or dynasty to which they belonged. Kings and princes were historically known by the names of the countries over which they and their families ruled. Therefore, royal family members only signed their first names (a tradition in the UK that continues to this day). There was a radical change in 1917 when George V specifically adopted Windsor, not only as the name of the house or dynasty but also as his family's family name. With this proclamation, he replaced the historic name of Saxe-Coburg-Gotha, and Windsor still remains the family name of today's royal family.

92. Who has a secret zip code?
A) The Sheriff of Nottingham
B) The inventor of the zip code
C) The President of the United States

The President of the United States.

The President of the United States receives approximately 60 to 80,000 letters a week. This is on top of the 100,000 emails and thousands of phone calls that come in every day. All correspondence sent to the President is processed, and due to the amount of mail sent to the White House, it is difficult for the President to receive personal mail. A letter sent to the White House by a personal friend or family member of the President would go through all necessary reviews before potentially being forwarded to staff who could, at best, forward the letter to a Secretary of the President. It is unlikely that the President will ever see a letter through these channels. But presidents have personal friends as well; they have family members who want to mail Christmas cards, they have bill collectors, and they need mail from outside the White House bubble. That's why the US Postal Service sets a secret personal zip code for the President's use. The President's personal zip code is shared with people he wishes to receive mail from during his time at the White House–a sort of VIP list for letters. If the secret zip code is somehow leaked, the postal service will issue a new one.

93. Who invented ice pops?
A) An 11-year-old entrepreneur
B) A 41-year-old entrepreneur
C) A 71-year-old entrepreneur

An 11-year-old entrepreneur.

Back in 1905, a kid from the San Francisco Bay Area named Frank Epperson accidentally invented the summer snack. He had mixed some sugary soda powder with water and left it outside overnight. It was a cold night, and the mixture froze. In the morning, Epperson gobbled up the icy concoction and licked it off the wooden stirrer. He called it "Epsicle," a word made up of icicles and his name, and began selling the treat in his neighborhood. In 1923, Epperson decided to expand sales beyond his neighborhood. He began selling the treat at Neptune Beach, a nearby amusement park. Neptune prospered in the days before the Depression, and consumers eagerly consumed Epsicles. Spurred by this success, Epperson applied for a patent in 1924 for his "frozen confection of attractive appearance which can be conveniently eaten without contamination by touching with the hand and without the necessity of a plate, spoon, fork or other utensils."

94. How much was Neil Armstrong's hair illegally sold for?

A) It was sold for $3,000
B) It was sold for $30,000
C) It was sold for $300,000

It was sold for $3,000.

Apollo moon mission astronaut Neil Armstrong has threatened to sue a barbershop owner who sold the space traveler's hair for $3,000. The buyer, John Reznikoff, said that he would not return the locks but would donate the purchase price to charity. He is a collector listed by the Guinness World Records as the largest collection of hair by historical celebrities. His collection, which is insured for $1 million, includes hair from Abraham Lincoln, Marilyn Monroe, Albert Einstein, and Napoleon. The barber, Marx Sizemore, received a letter from the former astronaut's attorney claiming the sale violated an Ohio law designed to protect the rights of famous people. The letter threatens legal action if Sizemore doesn't return the hair or doesn't use his winnings for charity and asks him to pay Armstrong's legal expenses. But Sizemore said he won't pay and has already spent most of the $3,000 on bills. Uff!

95. What grade did Martin Luther King Jr. get in public speaking at seminary school?

A) He got an A

B) He got a B

C) He got a C

He got a C.

Although King is undoubtedly an example of the greatest speakers of the English language of the 20th century, he once showed little academic promise in this department. It is hard to believe that the man who would become the most prolific public speaker of our time, who would deliver the "I Have A Dream speech," could come close to failing a public speaking course. But in his first year of seminary school in Chester, Pennsylvania, one of King's professors gave him a C in the public speaking course! He definitely practiced and improved because, in his third and final year, King was valedictorian with straight A's.

96. Who stated that pigeon poop was their property?

A) Queen Margrethe II of Denmark

B) King George I of England

C) King Carl XVI Gustav of Sweden

King George I of England.

Although pigeon poo is seen as a major problem for property owners in the 21st century, it was considered an invaluable resource in Europe in the 16th, 17th, and 18th centuries. Pigeon poop was a highly valued fertilizer and was thought to be far more effective than farmyard manure. In fact, it was so valued that armed guards were stationed at the entrances to dovecotes (pigeon houses) to stop thieves from stealing them. Not only that, but in England in the 16th century, pigeon poo was the only known source of saltpeter, an essential component of gunpowder, so King George I confirmed that the droppings were owned by the Crown.

97. Who won the 2015 French-language Scrabble World Championship?

A) A native New Zealander who speaks French

B) A native New Zealander who doesn't speak French

C) A native New Zealander who is blind

A native New Zealander who doesn't speak French.
Nigel Richards' Scrabble career went from great to astounding the week after winning the French-speaking Scrabble World Championships. The native New Zealander had already won several English language titles, and his new victory followed weeks of studying a French dictionary. How was he able to do that? Basically, he looked at word lists and dictionary pages, conjured up the picture of what he's seen, and that's enough for him to remember it. French Scrabble has 386,000 words. That's a lot—way more than North American Scrabble, which has 187,000 words. But the game isn't just about remembering words, it's a game of strategy and spatial relationships on the board, but Nigel seems to master it all.

98. Which American President was a licensed bartender?

A) Abraham Lincoln

B) Theodore Roosevelt

C) John F. Kennedy

Abraham Lincoln.
Lincoln was a co-owner of "Berry and Lincoln," a drinking

establishment that he founded with his friend William F. Berry. It was located in New Salem, Illinois, where he lived from 1831 to 1837. Stores could sell alcohol in quantities greater than 1 pint (half a liter) for off-premises consumption, but it was illegal to sell individual drinks to consume at the store without a license. In March 1833, Berry and Lincoln obtained a tavern license for $7 so they could serve half-pints (24 centiliters) of French brandy for 25 cents and other liquors for ridiculous prices. Unfortunately (or maybe fortunately), Lincoln's foray into the world of booze was short-lived. Berry was apparently an alcoholic and took advantage of the new license to drink while working in the store, which is why they went into debt.

99. Which famous musician did not know how to multiply?

A) Ludwig van Beethoven
B) Wolfgang Amadeus Mozart
C) Johann Sebastian Bach

Ludwig van Beethoven.

Beethoven was a virtuoso pianist from a young age and toured Europe with great success before becoming deaf in his late twenties/early thirties. Despite this seemingly debilitating illness, Beethoven continued to compose some of the greatest works of the Classical and Romantic periods and embodied the epitome of the human spirit of perseverance. Although being one of the most brilliant brains in the world, he wasn't able to multiply or divide. Because Beethoven had left school at the age of eleven to help with the household income, he never learned. For example, if he had to multiply "30 x 52," he would lay out thirty 52 times and add them up.

100. How much did Percy Spencer, the inventor of the microwave, receive for his discovery?
A) $2
B) $200
C) $2,000

Only $2.
When the product hit the market in 1947, weighing 750 pounds and costing over $2,000, it was a flop. Spencer had over 300 patents but received only $2 as a bonus for his invention. In 1999, he was immortalized for his invention and was inducted into the National Inventors Hall of Fame, which honors other famous inventors such as Thomas Edison and the Wright Brothers.

101. Which American president owned a pet hyena?
A) Abraham Lincoln
B) Benjamin Harrison
C) Theodore Roosevelt

Theodore Roosevelt.
Theodore Roosevelt and his family had many pets during their lifetime and were known to be great animal lovers. When the world learned of the family's love for animals, diplomatic leaders began sending exotic animals as gifts. Among them was a hyena named Bill. Bill was a gift to President Roosevelt from Emperor Menelik II of Ethiopia. Some sources say that Roosevelt loved this particular hyena and even allowed him to live in the White House for a while. In the end, Bill was sent to the National Zoo along with Joe the Lion to live out the remainder of their days.

102. What did the poet T.S. Eliot always wear on his face?

A) Mascara

B) Eyeliner

C) Green makeup

Green makeup.

After T. S. Eliot wrote The Waste Land, he started wearing green-tinted face powder. No one knew why he was doing it, but there were several rumors. The English art critic Clive Bell, for example, said he thought Eliot powdered his face to look "interesting and cadaverous." His biographer Peter Ackroyd agreed: Wearing face powder made Eliot feel more modern, more interesting, more of a poet than a bank clerk.

103. Who designed the current American flag?

A) An 11-year-old student

B) A 17-year-old student

C) A 23-year-old student

A 17-year-old student named Robert Heft.

Heft's teacher challenged his students to design a new 50-star flag after Hawaii and Alaska joined the Union. Robert designed it with 5 rows of six stars and 4 rows of five stars and spent 12.5 hours sewing the flag. His teacher thought the design was unoriginal and graded it a B but offered to give him an A if the design was nationally recognized. Heft accepted the challenge and contacted the White House. Two years later, his school project was selected as the national flag.

7 Bonus Questions

1. Mickey, Minnie, Donald Duck, Pinocchio, and other Disney characters all have one accessory in common: gloves. Do you know why?

To keep the animation easier.
Animation is an exhausting process. It takes time and extreme precision to create the characters we now know. Animators wanted to make their job easier and faster with a few techniques and hacks. One of these strategies was to use rounded edges instead of angles. This also meant simplifying functions like hands to speed up the animation process.

2. What is the first number that contains the letter A?

Just keep counting, you'll find out.
I'm kidding, this would take too long... the answer is one thousand. Although A is second in the number of appearances in the Concise Oxford English Dictionary, it is nowhere to be found in the English spellings of the first 999 numbers. Every other vowel appears (including Y). But A is not the last letter that appears when counting. The first number that contains a Q is one quadrillion, and for P it's one septillion!

They sleep on waterbeds.

As expected, Queen Elizabeth's 165 dairy cows are treated royally. Not only do they wander around and graze in huge green pastures, but they can also rub up against an automatic cow brush that removes dirt and relieves stress. Meanwhile, robots milk the cows and clean the floors, which means the cattle can come in in their own time rather than being left to the whims of a human milk farmer. But perhaps the greatest luxury the cattle enjoy is the water beds. The cows lie down on large pillows of water to sleep, but they also like to hang out on them during the day. As the cow lies down, the water pushes below where the cow lies, and they end up floating. Sounds positively dreamy! We may have to revisit the 70s and get our own waterbeds.

4. What bizarre injury did Brad Pitt sustain on the set of Troy?

Ironically, an Achilles tendon injury.

Pitt made an effort to get fit for the character of Achilles. As he admitted in an interview prior to the film's release, he worked hard for six months to get in shape. He ate 4 high-protein meals a day, exercised to build a lot of strength, and also kept carbohydrates to a minimum. However, all of his training couldn't stop him from inflicting an injury to his Achilles tendon while filming. The injury suspended filming for several weeks while Pitt recovered enough to resume production. While the film didn't get the best of reviews when it was released, there was no doubt that Pitt certainly looked like Achilles—injured foot and everything.

For $1.
James Cameron was not considered trustworthy as a director because of the failure of Piranha II (his previous movie). Nobody wanted him to direct the film, but he received many offers for the script from studios that were not interested in hiring him to direct. Although some of the offers involved large sums of money, he turned them all down. According to Cameron, the idea for the script came to him in a dream, and he was very attached to it. Eventually, he struck a deal with his co-writer, Hurd. Cameron would sell her full rights to the script for a dollar, on the condition that he could direct the film. Hurd agreed to Cameron's deal, and while Cameron got his wish to be the director of The Terminator, the post-release success probably made him completely regret his decision.

6. Is it possible to hum while holding your nose?

I bet you just tried it out, but no, it's not.
Why is this so? Because when you hum, you actually exhale. So when both your mouth and nose are closed, the air cannot escape. Although you can hum for a second or two, you will be forced to open your mouth and catch your breath.

7. Why does NASA use countdowns for the rocket launch?

Because of the science fiction pioneer Fritz Lang.
With countdown clocks, technicians and astronauts can synchronize their movements during a rocket launch sequence

from T-minus 43 hours until final ignition. However, their appeal goes way beyond practicality. The clock also serves as the visual version of a whistling teakettle, so viewers can ramp up their excitement as launch time draws nearer. When those last seconds pass before the start, it is dramatic, emotional–even cinematic. Which makes sense given the fact that the countdown clock for the rocket launch was not invented by meticulous engineers but by the filmmaker Fritz Lang. Although some previous novels and films used count-ups, the "Die Frau im Mond" movie was the first time the rocket met the countdown. Since then, they have been inseparable.

Conclusion

We are already at the end of our adventure, and I hope you enjoyed this fun trivia quiz. Probably, you won't remember most of the facts but don't let this stop you from staying curious and learning more.

That being said, how did you like the book? Let me know by leaving a review. You can click right here or scan the code below. It only takes 30 seconds, and this would really help me out. I'm sending greetings to you in advance!

Amazon.com/review/create-review?&asin=B0BMYVZX7F

Thank you so much, I wish you only the best!

Sources

6 Famous Discontinued and Uncommon U.S. Currency Denominations. (2020, September 9). Investopedia. https://www.investopedia.com/6-famous-discontinued-and-uncommon-u-s-currency-denominations-4773302#:%7E:-text=The%20Bureau%20of%20Engraving%20and%20Printing%20created%20them%20during%20the,%24100%2C000%20bills%20were%20ever%20printed.

The 10 Greatest Empires In The History Of The World. (2017, May 12). Business Insider. https://www.businessinsider.com/the-10-greatest-empires-in-history-2011-9?r=US&IR=T#1-the-british-empire-was-the-largest-empire-the-world-has-ever-seen-10

11 Things You Might Not Know About Giraffes. (2020, November 11). Treehugger. https://www.treehugger.com/giraffe-facts-5072826#:%7E:text=Much%20like%20their%20necks%2C%20giraffe,and%20shoots%20into%20their%20mouths

A. (2020a, September 3). *Brad Pitt's on-set injury on "Troy" is a strange tribute to his character Achilles*. FR24 News. https://www.fr24news.com/a/2020/09/brad-pitts-on-set-injury-on-troy-is-a-strange-tribute-to-his-character-achilles.html

Aimee, A. (2014, November 14). *Why McDonald's created bubble gum-flavored broccoli*. CBS News. https://www.cbsnews.com/news/why-mcdonalds-created-bubble-gum-flavored-broccoli/

Animal Facts - Lobsters. (n.d.). Vegan Peace. https://www.veganpeace.com/animal_facts/Lobsters.htm#:%7E:text=The%20four%20small%20antennae%20on,and%20to%20watch%20for%20enemies

Baby giant South American river turtles talk to each other from inside eggs. (2014, August 29). CBC. https://www.cbc.ca/news/science/baby-giant-south-american-river-turtles-talk-to-each-other-from-inside-eggs-1.2747542

Barrabi, T. (2020, June 18). *Rare Nike "waffle iron" shoes could fetch $150K at auction*. Fox Business. https://www.foxbusiness.com/sports/nike-waffle-iron-shoes-bill-bowerman-auction

Bartender-In-Chief: Abraham Lincoln Owned A Tavern. (2013, February 12). The Chicagoist. https://chicagoist.com/2013/02/12/abraham_lincoln_bartender.php#:%7E:text=Back%20before%20he%20was%20President%2C%20Abraham%20Lincoln%20was%20a%20lawyer.&tex-

t=But%20Lincoln%20was%20the%20only,lived%20from%201831%20 to%201837.+https://www.wannafactph.com/2020/07/pigeon-poop-crown.html

Baseball umpires used to sit in rocking chairs. (n.d.). NTKF. https://www.need-toknowfacts.com/sports/baseball-umpires-used-to-sit-in-rocking-chairs

Bates, M. (2021, May 3). *Picky Pigs Take Washing Certain Foods Seriously.* Animals. https://www.nationalgeographic.com/animals/article/151023-wild-boar-pigs-wash-food-animals-behavior-science#:%7E:text=Cleaning%20 Up,and%20primates%20all%20do%20so.

BBC - Ouch! (disability) - Fact - Ouch Q&A: HÃ©ctor Castro 1930s disabled football star. (2007, June 7). BBC. https://www.bbc.co.uk/ouch/fact/ q_a_h_ctor_castro_1930s_disabled_football_star.shtml

BBC News. (2015, September 23). *Scots "have 421 words" for snow.* https:// www.bbc.com/news/uk-scotland-34323967#:%7E:text=Scotland%20 has%20more%20than%20400,%22%20(a%20large%20snowflake).

Beach, J. (2019, April 9). *10 crazy traffic laws you didn't know you were breaking as a cyclist.* BikeRadar. https://www.bikeradar.com/featu-res/10-crazy-traffic-laws-you-didnt-know-you-were-breaking-as-a-cyc-list/#:%7E:text=5.,riding%20in%20Galesburg%2C%20Illinois%2C%20 USA&text=It's%20true%2C%20we've%20looked,fancy%20riding%20 on%20any%20street.%E2%80%9D

Beefalo. (n.d.). American Beefalo Association. http://americanbeefaloassociation. com/benefits

Booth, J. (2019, January 25). *McDonald's Sells A McSpaghetti Dinner Meal, And Here's Where You Can Get It.* So Yummy. https://soyummy.com/mcdon-alds-unexpected-dinner-meal/

Browne, R. (2019, November 25). *Web creator Tim Berners-Lee launches plan to "fix" the internet.* CNBC. https://www.cnbc.com/2019/11/25/tim-bern-ers-lee-launches-contract-for-the-web-to-fix-the-internet.html

Bryner, M. (2010, August 23). *What's the Biggest Animal in the World?* Live-science.Com. https://www.livescience.com/32780-whats-the-biggest-animal-in-the-world.html#:%7E:text=Its%20tongue%20alone%20 weighs%205%2C400,the%20largest%20babies%20on%20earth.

CBS News. (2011, January 5). *15 Most Bizarre Medical Treatments Ever.* https:// www.cbsnews.com/pictures/15-most-bizarre-medical-treatments-ever/2/

D. (2014a, March 1). *The President's Secret ZIP Code.* Dead Presidents. https://deadpresidents.tumblr.com/post/78147000455/the-presidents-secret-zip-code

Dearden, L. (2017, August 4). *Bulletproof armadillo puts Texas man in hospital after shot bounces off hard shell.* The Independent. https://www.independent.co.uk/news/world/americas/bulletproof-armadillo-puts-texas-man-hospital-after-shot-bounces-hard-shell-10432102.html

Deutsche Welle (www.dw.com). (n.d.). *A group of ravens makes a. . .* DW.COM. https://www.dw.com/en/what-do-you-call-a-group-of-ravens/a-18221414

Dhanaraj, J. (2016, November 23). *Woman calls police, upset over lack of sprinkles on ice cream.* The New Paper. https://tnp.straitstimes.com/news/woman-calls-police-upset-over-lack-sprinkles-ice-cream

DiNuzzo, E. (2019, April 10). *This Is Why Most Disney Characters Wear Gloves.* Reader's Digest. https://www.rd.com/article/why-do-disney-characters-wear-gloves/

Fernando, G. (2017, January 9). *What the hell does 'OK' stand for?* News. https://www.news.com.au/technology/science/evolution/what-the-hell-does-ok-stand-for/news-story/e65a0bad16107c887f97356e680329fc#:%7E:text=It's%20more%20correct%20to%20write,%2C%20or%20%E2%80%9Call%20correct%E2%80%9D.

Figuring Out the Largest Animal with NO Teeth! (n.d.). Science Bug Blog. http://sciencebug.org/blog/tag/blue-whale-facts/#:~:text=Scientists%20in%20Canada%20estimated%20that,pound%20(150%20ton)%20body!

Five interesting facts on the birthday of Martin Luther King Jr. (n.d.). The National Constitution Center. https://constitutioncenter.org/interactive-constitution/blog/five-interesting-facts-about-dr-martin-luther-king-jr-2#:%7E:text=Fact%201%3A%20King%20got%20a,public%20speaking%20at%20seminary%20school.&text=But%20in%20his%20first%20year,was%20valedictorian%20with%20straight%20A's.

Fries, W. C. (2009, July 17). *Cats and Dairy: Get the Facts.* WebMD. https://pets.webmd.com/cats/guide/cats-and-dairy-get-the-facts#1

Gaskill, M. (2018, October 24). *Roller Coasters were First Invented to Distract People from Immoral Behavior.* The Vintage News. https://www.thevintagenews.com/2018/10/24/roller-coasters/

Generator, M. (n.d.). *Humanimalia.* Humanimalia. https://humanimalia.org/

Giaimo, C. (2016, February 27). *NASA Stole the Rocket Countdown From a 1929 Fritz Lang Film*. Atlas Obscura. https://www.atlasobscura.com/articles/nasa-stole-the-rocket-countdown-from-a-1929-fritz-lang-film-1d569cc0-50ff-4045-b0c9-1f0d72a193db

Grundhauser, E. (2016, February 28). *The Dunce Cap Wasn't Always So Stupid*. Atlas Obscura. https://www.atlasobscura.com/articles/the-dunce-cap-wasnt-always-so-stupid#:%7E:text=The%20dunce%20cap%20has%20long,a%20symbol%20of%20respected%20scholars.

Higgins, E. (2021, October 22). *What Did People Do Before Toilet Paper?* Farmers' Almanac. https://www.farmersalmanac.com/before-toilet-paper-24419

The History Of Glitter. (n.d.). The Ransom Note. https://www.theransomnote.com/music/young-marco-takeover/the-history-of-glitter/

How Cows Eat Grass. (2021, August 18). U.S. Food and Drug Administration. https://www.fda.gov/animal-veterinary/animal-health-literacy/how-cows-eat-grass

I. (2014b, March 20). *Did you know you can't hold your nose and hum?* DiamondWellness.Com. https://diamondwellness.com/802/#:%7E:text=It%20is%20because%20when%20you,mouth%20and%20catch%20your%20breath.

Inge, S. (2015, May 5). *Italian astronaut has first espresso in space*. The Local Italy. https://www.thelocal.it/20150505/italian-astronaut-has-first-espresso-in-space

It's Flag Day. Here are some fun facts about the American flag you may not have known. (2020, June 14). FOX10 News. https://www.fox10tv.com/news/us_world_news/its-flag-day-here-are-some-fun-facts-about-the-american-flag-you-may-not/article_b1da5d64-12d4-5a87-9138-fb9d653f2cfc.html

Jain, S. (2019, October 16). *Why Do Passports Only Come In Four Colours?* NDTV.Com. https://www.ndtv.com/offbeat/why-do-passports-only-come-in-four-colours-2117697

Jones, M. (2019, April 4). *You Can Spell Every Number Up to 1,000 Without This Common Letter*. Reader's Digest. https://www.rd.com/article/spell-number-up-1000-without-a/

Jones, M. (2021a, July 16). *There's Only One Letter That's Not in Any U.S. State*

Name. Can You Guess It? Reader's Digest. https://www.rd.com/article/letter-not-in-any-state-name/

Jones, M. (2021b, July 19). *This Is the Only U.S. State Capital Without a Single McDonald's.* Reader's Digest. https://www.rd.com/article/state-capital-without-mcdonalds/

Joy, A. (2019, August 28). *"Albert Einstein" Is an Anagram for "Ten Elite Brains."* World Baba. https://worldbaba.blogspot.com/2019/08/albert-einstein-is-anagram-for-ten.html

Labor Pains. (n.d.). Slate Magazine. https://slate.com/gdpr?redirect_uri=%2Farticles%2Farts%2Fpoem%2F2010%2F01%2Flabor_pains.html%3Fvia%3Dgdpr-consent&redirect_host=http%3A%2F%2Fwww.slate.com

Laliberte, M. (2018, June 6). *The Weird Reason Queen Elizabeth II's Cows Use Waterbeds.* Reader's Digest. https://www.rd.com/article/queen-elizabeth-cow-waterbeds/

Laliberte, M., & Taylor-Smith, J. (2021, October 13). *100 Fun and Interesting Facts About Practically Everything.* Reader's Digest. https://www.rd.com/list/interesting-facts/

Lambrechts, S. (2018, November 8). *Samsung built a robot butt just to test its smartphones' durability.* TechRadar. https://www.techradar.com/news/samsung-built-a-robot-butt-just-to-test-its-smartphones-durability

Leasca, S. (2018, October 20). *A Sloth Can Hold Its Breath for 40 Minutes Underwater — and 6 Other Facts For International Sloth Day.* Travel + Leisure. https://www.travelandleisure.com/animals/international-sloth-day

Locker, M. (2014, January 21). *Breaking Breakfast News: Froot Loops Are All the Same Flavor.* Time. https://time.com/1477/breaking-breakfast-news-froot-loops-are-all-the-same-flavor/

M. (n.d.). *How Long Can A Dolphin Hold Its Breath?* Ponce Inlet Watersports. https://ponceinletwatersports.com/how-long-can-a-dolphin-hold-its-breath/#:%7E:text=On%20average%2C%20dolphins%20can%20hold,oxygen%20needed%20to%20stay%20underwater

M.A. (2013a, October 11). *William McKinley Gave Away His Good Luck Charm (And Died).* KnowledgeNuts. https://knowledgenuts.com/2013/10/11/william-mckinley-gave-away-his-good-luck-charm-and-died/

MacRae, G. (2020, October 26). *Queen Elizabeth II has very own "body double" in bombshell 30 year Royal Family secret*. Express.Co.Uk. https://www.express.co.uk/news/royal/1352219/queen-elizabeth-II-body-double-melania-trump-royal-family-ella-slack-latest-updates-ont

Magazine, S. (n.d.). *Bananas Are Berries?* STANFORD Magazine. https://stanfordmag.org/contents/bananas-are-berries

Magazine, S. (2013a, May 1). *Never Underestimate the Power of a Paint Tube*. Smithsonian Magazine. https://www.smithsonianmag.com/arts-culture/never-underestimate-the-power-of-a-paint-tube-36637764/

Magazine, S. (2013b, June 18). *Why the Tomato Was Feared in Europe for More Than 200 Years*. Smithsonian Magazine. https://www.smithsonianmag.com/arts-culture/why-the-tomato-was-feared-in-europe-for-more-than-200-years-863735/#:%7E:text=In%20the%20late%201700s%2C%20a,were%20high%20in%20lead%20content

Martínez, M. (2020, September 17). *These five countries have no airport (because there's no space)*. Ferrovial's Blog. https://blog.ferrovial.com/en/2018/04/these-five-countries-have-no-airport-because-theres-no-space/#:%7E:text=But%20there%20are%20a%20few,Vatican%20are%20States%20without%20airports.

Mercado, M. (2019, January 31). *Most Wasabi Isn't Real Wasabi, Which Is Actually Way More Rare & Expensive Than You Think*. Bustle. https://www.bustle.com/p/most-wasabi-isnt-real-wasabi-which-is-actually-way-more-rare-expensive-than-you-think-15914765#:%7E:text=Wasabi%20plants%20require%20very%20specific,don't%20know%20until%20now.

Merelli, A. (2016, October 7). *Adolf Hitler was nominated for the Nobel Peace Prize in a darkly ironic letter by Erik Gottfrid Christian Brandt*. Quartz. https://qz.com/803976/adolf-hitler-was-nominated-for-the-nobel-peace-prize-in-a-darkly-ironic-letter-by-erik-gottfrid-christian-brandt/

Mowke, D. (2016, December 30). *Which is the biggest single-celled organism?* Inshorts - Stay Informed. https://inshorts.com/en/news/which-is-the-biggest-singlecelled-organism-1483102816516

Mulraney, F. (2021, March 2). *All the pubs in Ireland used to be closed on St. Patrick's Day*. IrishCentral.Com. https://www.irishcentral.com/roots/history/all-pubs-ireland-closed-st-patricks-day

Muto, J. (2017, June 16). *What does H&M stand for?* TODAY.Com. https://www.today.com/style/what-does-h-m-stand-t112815

My Modern Met. (2017, August 1). *World's Oldest Bottle of Wine Remains Unopened Since the 4th Century*. https://mymodernmet.com/oldest-unopened-bottle-wine-world/#:%7E:text=So%2C%20how%20old%20is%20the,tomb%20in%20modern%2Dday%20Germany.

N. (2013b, May 1). *Uncommon Knowledge: What was the last letter added to the alphabet?* -. The Goods. https://www.uncommongoods.com/blog/2013/uncommon-knowledge-letter-added-alphabet/

The National Park - The world's biggest national park - [Visit Greenland!]. (2021a, May 11). Visit Greenland. https://visitgreenland.com/the-national-park/

The National Park - The world's biggest national park - [Visit Greenland!]. (2021b, May 11). Visit Greenland. https://visitgreenland.com/the-national-park/

NBC Universal. (2005, June 2). *Astronaut's hair sparks legal hubbub*. NBC News. https://www.nbcnews.com/id/wbna8062442

NPR Cookie Consent and Choices. (2011, June 2). Npr. https://choice.npr.org/index.html?origin=https://www.npr.org/sections/krulwich/2011/06/02/136860918/the-hardest-working-mom-on-the-planet?t=1610718604047

NPR Cookie Consent and Choices. (2015a, July 21). Npr. https://choice.npr.org/index.html?origin=https://www.npr.org/sections/thetwo-way/2015/07/21/424980378/winner-of-french-scrabble-title-does-not-speak-french

NPR Cookie Consent and Choices. (2015b, July 22). Npr. https://choice.npr.org/index.html?origin=https://www.npr.org/sections/thesalt/2015/07/22/425294957/how-an-11-year-old-boy-invented-the-popsicle

O. (2019a, November 1). *Thanks to 3D printing, NASA can basically "email" tools to astronauts*. The Brain Maze. https://thebrainmaze.com/thanks-to-3-d-printing-nasa-can-basically-email-tools-to-astronauts/#:%7E:text=Technology-,Thanks%20to%203D%20printing%2C%20NASA,basically%20%E2%80%9Cemail%E2%80%9D%20tools%20to%20astronauts&text=Getting%20new%20equipment%20to%20the,a%20life%20or%20death%20matter.

Passy, J. (2019, October 21). *Here is the world's shortest (1.5 minutes) and longest (19.5 hours) commercial flight*. MarketWatch. https://www.marketwatch.

com/story/this-is-the-worlds-shortest-regularly-scheduled-flight-on-a-commercial-airline-2018-10-17#:%7E:text=Loganair%2C%20a%20Scottish%20regional%20airline,1.5%20minutes%20in%20the%20air.

Pez - The World's First Smoking Cessation Product. (2019, September 17). American Council on Science and Health. https://www.acsh.org/news/2019/09/16/pez-worlds-first-smoking-cessation-product-14284

Picard, C. (2021, August 14). *50 cool trivia facts to impress your friends*. Good Housekeeping. Retrieved October 26, 2021, from https://www.goodhousekeeping.com/life/g25692093/random-trivia/.

Pictures: Colored Honey Made by Candy-Eating French Bees. (2021, May 3). Animals. https://www.nationalgeographic.com/animals/article/121011-blue-honey-honeybees-animals-science#:%7E:-text=Pictures%3A%20Colored%20Honey%20Made%20by%20Candy%2DEating%20French%20Bees&text=Beekeepers%20in%20northeastern%20France%20found,blue%20and%20green%20(pictured).&text=This%20honeycomb%20shows%20some%20of,one%20of%20the%20French%20beehives

Poppick, L. (2014, February 5). *Bumblebees Can Fly Higher Than Mount Everest*. Livescience.Com. https://www.livescience.com/43114-bumble-bees-fly-higher-mount-everest.html#:%7E:text=Alpine%20bumblebees%20have%20the%20ability,Everest%2C%20scientists%20have%20found.&text=All%20of%20the%20bees%20were,the%20team%20reported%20Tuesday%20

Presidential Pet Museum. (n.d.). *Theodore Roosevelt's Hyena*. https://www.presidentialpetmuseum.com/theodore-roosevelts-hyena/

The Royal Family name. (2016, April 3). The Royal Family. https://www.royal.uk/royal-family-name

Rus, T. (2014, November 28). *Mercedes F200 Imagination: the joystick-controlled concept*. MercedesBlog. https://mercedesblog.com/mercedes-f200-imagination-joystick-controlled-vehicle/

Russell, M. (2018, July 9). *Meet The ManhattAnts: Unique Species Of Ant Found Only In New York City*. The Rainforest Site News. https://blog.therainforestsite.greatergood.com/manhattant-species/#:%7E:text=Thank%20you!-,Meet%20The%20ManhattAnts%3A%20Unique%20Species%20Of%20Ant,Only%20In%20New%20York%20City&text=%E2%80%9CIt's%20a%20relative%20of%20the,entirely%20new%20species%20of%20ant

Saraniero, N. (2021, October 26). *10 Secrets of Yonkers Raceway at Empire City Casino*. Untapped New York. https://untappedcities.com/2017/03/14/daily-what-einsteins-eyeballs-are-in-a-safety-deposit-box-in-nyc/

Saunders, M. (2019, July 4). *The real Tinkerbell: don't mess with these tiny fairy wasps*. The Conversation. https://theconversation.com/the-real-tinkerbell-dont-mess-with-these-tiny-fairy-wasps-109796#:%7E:text=The%20smallest%20known%20insect%20of,found%20in%20the%20United%20States.

Scales, H. (n.d.). *How many hearts does an octopus have?* BBC Science Focus Magazine. https://www.sciencefocus.com/nature/why-does-an-octopus-have-more-than-one-heart/

Sea Cucumber - Holothuroidea. (2017, July 6). The Shape of Life | The Story of the Animal Kingdom. https://www.shapeoflife.org/news/featured-creature/2017/06/30/sea-cucumber-holothuroidea

Seager, C. (2019, August 21). *Facepaint, champagne and antelope skin – writers' oddball quirks revealed*. The Guardian. https://www.theguardian.com/books/2015/jul/23/facepaint-champagne-and-antelope-skin-writers-oddball-quirks-revealed#:%7E:text=TS%20Eliot%20wore%20green%20makeup%20and%20lipstick%20when%20he%20wrote&text=Quite%20why%20he%20assumed%20a%20green%20pallor%2C%20nobody%20knew.&text=His%20biographer%2C%20Peter%20Ackroyd%2C%20agreed,rather%20than%20a%20bank%20official.%E2%80%9D

Sehra, S. (2016, June 16). *Eiffel Tower gets taller by 6 inches in summer*. Inshorts - Stay Informed. https://inshorts.com/en/news/eiffel-tower-gets-taller-by-6-inches-in-summer-1466096019720

Shamsian, J. (2019, July 2). *Here's why your pants have a teeny tiny pocket that's too small to use*. Insider. https://www.insider.com/small-pocket-pants-jeans-watch-2018-03

Sharp, T. (2018, May 22). *World's First Commercial Airline | The Greatest Moments in Flight*. Space.Com. https://www.space.com/16657-worlds-first-commercial-airline-the-greatest-moments-in-flight.html#:%7E:text=Pheil%2C%20former%20mayor%20of%20St,an%20aviation%20entrepreneur%20from%20St.

The shortest war in history: The Anglo-Zanzibar War of 1896. (n.d.). The Historical Association. https://www.history.org.uk/secondary/resource/7950/the-shortest-war-in-history-the-anglo-zanzibar-wa#:%7E:text=At%209am%20on%2027%20August,Palace%20and%20Harem%20in%20Zanzibar.

Should I Worry About How Hot My Engine Is Running? (n.d.). Cars.Com. https://www.cars.com/articles/should-i-worry-about-how-hot-my-engine-is-running-1420680334271/#:%7E:text=For%20most%20cars%2C%20the%20normal,normal%20range%20in%20the%20middle

Simpson, J. (2017, July 18). *The British Perfected the Art of Brewing Tea Inside an Armored Vehicle.* War Is Boring. https://warisboring.com/the-british-perfected-the-art-of-brewing-tea-inside-an-armored-vehicle/#:%7E:text=Tank%20crewmen%20had%20to%20stop,one%20disastrous%20World%20War%20II.

Sinha, S. (2020, November 5). *Microwave Was An Accident, And The Inventor Was Paid Only $2 For It!* Global Youth Voice. https://www.globalyouthvoice.com/microwave-oven/#:%7E:text=Spencer%20has%20over%20300%20patents,Edison%20and%20the%20Wright%20Brothers.

Staff, S. X. (2008, October 17). *Blue bananas: Ripening bananas glow an intense blue under black light.* Phys.Org. https://phys.org/news/2008-10-blue-bananas-ripening-intense-black.html#:%7E:text=Under%20normal%20light%2C%20these%20natural,ripening%20bananas%20appear%20blue%20instead.&text=The%20intensity%20of%20the%20luminescence,progress%2C%20the%20blue%20glow%20decreases

Stage, C. (2017, April 5). *Ludwig van Beethoven: An Overview.* Center Stage Music Center. https://centerstagemusiccenter.com/ludwig-van-beethoven-an-overview/

Stanek, B. (2017, May 24). *Scientists may have finally figured out how flamingos can stand on one leg, not fall over.* The Week. https://theweek.com/speedreads/701166/scientists-may-have-finally-figured-how-flamingos-stand-leg-not-fall-over

Statue of Liberty Lighthouse. (n.d.). LighthouseFriends. https://lighthousefriends.com/light.asp?ID=581

Sticking their necks out for evolution: Why sloths and manatees have unusually long (or short) necks. (n.d.). ScienceDaily. https://www.sciencedaily.com/releases/2011/05/110505212314.htm

The shortest railways in the world take less than a Minute. Best Travel Tale. (2020, February 21). Retrieved October 26, 2021, from https://besttraveltale.com/travel/the-shortest-railways-in-the-world-take-less-than-a-minute/.

The Swearing-In of the First Woman Elected to Congress, Representative Jeannette Rankin of Montana | US House of Representatives: History, Art & Archives. (n.d.). History, Art & Archives. https://history.house.gov/Historical-Highlights/1901-1950/The-swearing-in-of-the-first-woman-elected-to-Congress,-Representative-Jeannette-Rankin-of-Montana/

The Terminator: James Cameron's HUGE Mistake To Direct The Movie. (2020, January 29). Screen Rant. https://screenrant.com/terminator-movie-cameron-screenplay-sold-one-dollar/

U.T. (2014c, September 29). *USA TODAY*. Newser. https://eu.usatoday.com/story/news/nation/2014/09/29/secret-starbucks-cia/16430023/

V. (2020b, July 5). *Shell-shaped gas station in Winston-Salem, North Carolina*. Silly America. https://sillyamerica.com/blog/shell-shaped-gas-station-in-winston-salem-north-carolina/

Villazon, L. (n.d.). *Can a human produce a sound outside the human audible range?* BBC Science Focus Magazine. https://www.sciencefocus.com/the-human-body/can-a-human-produce-a-sound-outside-the-human-audible-range/#:%7E:text=But%20a%20few%20individuals%20have,t%20be%20heard%2C%20only%20felt.

W. (2019b, October 1). *How Many Balls Are Used at Wimbledon?* WDH. https://www.wimbledondebentureholders.com/articles/2019/10/01/how-many-balls-used-wimbledon/#:%7E:text=Because%20of%20the%20effect%20of,they%20aren't%20worn%20down.

Website, T. O. E. T. (2021, February 1). *How did they build the Tower so quickly?* La Tour Eiffel. https://www.toureiffel.paris/en/news/130-years/how-did-they-build-tower-so-quickly

Where is Earth's Largest Waterfall? (n.d.). National Ocean Service. https://oceanservice.noaa.gov/facts/largest-waterfall.html

Which Came First: Orange the Color or Orange the Fruit? (2012, February 8). Mental Floss. https://www.mentalfloss.com/article/29942/which-came-first-orange-color-or-orange-fruit

Your supermarket apples may be 10 months old. (2017, April 8). Business Insider. https://www.businessinsider.com/supermarket-apples-10-months-old-2017-4?r=US&IR=T#:%7E:text=That%20apple%20you%20just%20ate,harvested%20from%20August%20to%20November.&text=Apples%20that%20will%20be%20sold%20later%20go%20to%20controlled%20atmosphere%20storage.

(2015a, December 23). *Were Lunar Volcanoes Active When Dinosaurs Roamed the Earth?* Universe Today. https://www.universetoday.com/115245/were-lunar-volcanoes-active-when-dinosaurs-roamed-the-earth/

(2015b, December 24). *Why Are Lunar Shadows So Dark?* Universe Today. https://www.universetoday.com/93991/why-are-lunar-shadows-so-dark/#:%7E:text=On%20the%20Moon%20there%20is,where%20sunlight%20hits%2C%20very%20bright.&text=It%20tends%20to%20reflect%20light,seen%20in%20Apollo%20mission%20photographs.

Made in the USA
Monee, IL
29 November 2022

18853429R00127